Integrative Regulatory Therapy

A Multi-Focal Strategy for Cancer Control

Francisco Contreras, MD

Jorge Barroso-Aranda, MD, PhD

Mark F. McCarty

Integrative Regulatory Therapy - A Multi-Focal Strategy for Cancer Control
By Francisco Contreras, MD, Jorge Barroso-Aranda, MD, PhD,
and Mark F. McCarty.
Published by Oasis of Hope Press
1685 Precision Park Lane, Suite L
San Diego, CA 92173
Tel. (619) 428-0930
Fax. (619) 428-0994

Publisher & Editor: Daniel E. Kennedy
Researchers & Contributors: Francisco Contreras, MD,
Jorge Barroso-Aranda, MD, PhD, Mark F. McCarty, Daniel E. Kennedy,
Leticia Wong, and Bruce Northey.
Additional Support: Shary Oden
Cover Design/Graphic Design/Formatting: Viviana Flores

International Standard Book Number: 978-1-57946-008-2

This book is not intended to provide medical advice or to take the place of medical advice and treatment from your personal physician. Readers are advised to consult their own doctors or other qualified health professionals regarding the treatment of their medical problems. Neither the publisher nor the authors take any responsibility for any possible consequences from any treatment, action or application of medicine, supplement, herb or preparation to any person reading or following information in this book. If readers are taking prescription medications, again, they should consult with their physicians and not take themselves off of medicines to start supplementations or a nutrition program without the proper supervision of a physician.

Printed in the United States of America

Introduction

■ ■ ■

In 1963, the late Dr. Ernesto Contreras, Sr. opened the Oasis of Hope Hospital and initiated what would become a healing tradition known as the Total Care Approach. Dr. Contreras is recognized in multiple publications as a pioneer in body, mind, and spirit medicine. At the foundation of his philosophy were two principles inspired by Hippocrates, the father of medicine, and Jesus Christ, The Great Physician: 1) First, do no harm; 2) Love your patient as you love yourself.

Because of his philosophy, Dr. Contreras taught his medical staff to never prescribe treatments that would destroy the quality of life of the patient. He also insisted that Oasis of Hope physicians offer therapies that they would be willing to take if in the same circumstances. His emphasis on the doctor-patient relationship, along with his integration of natural and conventional therapies with emotional and spiritual counseling, were the principle reasons why more than 100,000 patients from 55 nations have come to Oasis of Hope for treatment over the last 45 years.

Dr. Contreras believed that to be effective as a physician, one had to blend art and science. When treating cancer patients, Dr. Contreras looked beyond the obvious. He would find the root needs of his patients and develop personalized therapies to address the unique circumstance of each. His commitment to treat his patients with professionalism, ethics, and compassion made him a beloved doctor. As a researcher, Dr. Contreras explored hundreds of treatment modalities in his constant quest to help his patients. His untiring determination inspired his staff and patients alike.

At age 88, after 62 years of medical practice, Dr. Contreras went on to be with the Lord. Two of his significant contributions to humanity were his model for integrative medicine and the development of a tremendous platform for the advancement of cancer research, treatment, and control. The Oasis of Hope is home of the healing legacy of Dr. Ernesto Contreras, Sr. and the staff continues to utilize the Total Care Approach and develop and design new and effective protocols for comprehensive cancer management.

Oasis of Hope practitioners are not satisfied with the traditional goal of oncology, which is tumor destruction. When reviewing cancer survival rates, it becomes apparent that focusing solely on tumor destruction is not sufficient. This book proposes a new set of treatment goals, medical protocols, and ideologies. It outlines a unique cancer treatment approach that has been developed by the Oasis of Hope Clinical Research Organization under the leadership of oncologist Francisco Contreras, MD; Jorge Barroso-Aranda, MD, PhD; and Mark F. McCarty. The Oasis of Hope founder and his successors have championed goals that are much more effective, sophisticated and profound than the traditional emphasis on direct tumor destruction.

The explanation of the scientific basis for cancer treatment at Oasis of Hope, and the review of results that are presented in this book, support the premise that cancer treatment must be integrative and multi-disciplinary, and that the efficacy of chemotherapy, radiation, and surgery increases when used in conjunction with nutraceuticals, diet, exercise, counseling, and spiritual support.

This book is written as an entry-level medical publication with the intention of inspiring further study and practice of integrative cancer management protocols. It embraces Dr. Ernesto Contreras, Sr.'s vision of treating the whole person, and it demonstrates how to effectively integrate conventional medicine, nutraceuticals, diet, exercise, counseling, and spiritual support. After reading this book, please visit www.oasisofhope.com/whitepapers to find more information about Oasis of Hope therapies.

–Daniel E. Kennedy
Chief Executive Officer
Oasis of Hope Health Group

About the Authors

■ ■ ■

Francisco Contreras, MD is Oasis of Hope's Chairman and President. He is the son of Oasis of Hope's founder, Dr. Ernesto Contreras, Sr.. Dr. Contreras specialized in surgical oncology at the University of Vienna, Austria, and has led the Oasis of Hope since 1983. Dr. Contreras has authored 12 books and lectures regularly at universities and conferences throughout the United States, Mexico, Central and South America, Europe, and Asia.

Jorge Barroso-Aranda, MD, PhD is Oasis of Hope's Vice-President of Medicine and Research. He has a Bachelor of Science in engineering. He is an MD, who also completed a PhD in biomedical engineering at the University of California San Diego (UCSD). He also received the degree of Postdoctoral Fellow in biomedical engineering from UCSD. From 1992 to 1996, Dr. Barroso-Aranda served as Director of the Environmental Protection Agency for the state of Baja California, Mexico. Dr. Barroso-Aranda has worked on numerous research studies with Dr. Benjamin W. Zweifach, considered to be the "father of microcirculation." Dr. Barroso-Aranda is widely published in medical journals.

Mark F. McCarty is a nutritionist and a researcher who obtained his undergraduate education in biochemistry at the University of California San Diego, Revelle College. He has published over two hundred articles on a wide range of biomedical topics in the peer-reviewed medical literature. He has been awarded seven U.S. patents for a variety of applied nutritional measures. McCarty co-founded NutriGuard Research and worked for many years as the research director for Nutrition 21. He brings his expertise in nutrition and his research experience to the Oasis of Hope Clinical Research Organization.

Preface

■ ■ ■

"My people perish for lack of knowledge," wrote the prophet Hosea. How true this is in the arena of cancer. For that reason, continual education – of ourselves, of our patients, and of society at large – is a paramount commitment of the Oasis of Hope Health Group. Finding practical ways to avoid and control the scourge of cancer is the chief focus of these efforts.

As is well known, the risk for developing specific types of cancer by a given age is quite often a function of modifiable lifestyle factors. More and more, epidemiology suggests that one can greatly lower the risk for certain cancers by measures such as: 1) Adopting a quasi-vegan diet low in fatty animal products. This diet includes an ample intake of fruits and cruciferous vegetables such as cabbage, broccoli, and cauliflower. It also includes vegetables rich in alliums such as garlic and onions; 2) Maintaining leanness and good insulin sensitivity with regular exercise and smart eating habits; 3) Achieving good vitamin D status and optimal selenium nutrition; 4) Avoiding overt mutagens such as tobacco smoke or excessive sun exposure.

Nonetheless, the probability of developing some life-threatening form of cancer is significant, even if every feasible effort is taken to lower one's risk. That's not true for a number of the other dangerous disorders that afflict Western society. At least until recently, coronary heart disease and diabetes have been virtually unheard of in many cultures where the traditional diets are low in fatty animal products and an active lifestyle helps to keep people lean. Stroke, and even Alzheimer's disease, seem to be quite rare wherever people have eaten an unsalted diet most their lives.

Conversely, thanks largely to clean water, sanitation, and vaccination programs, people in the First World now enjoy substantial protection from infectious disorders such as smallpox, cholera, typhus, the plague, and tuberculosis that wiped out tens of millions of people in past centuries. But cancer has been an uncontrolled threat for centuries, and continues to be. The "inevitability" of cancer as one ages, reflects the fact that mutations gradually accumulate in body cells that have replicative potential (stem cells) – and sooner or later, these mutations will give rise to colonies of rogue cells that evade normal growth control mechanisms, and eventually gain the ability to spread unchecked throughout the body. Unfortunately, cancer is an equal opportunity offender that respects no gender, age or social status.

Hoping for "the cure" is not recommended. That's because cancer isn't just one disease – it's a family of hundreds of diseases. Within each histological type of cancer, each person's individual case of cancer is distinct – the cells in one person's breast cancer are bio-chemically distinct from another person's breast cancer. Since cancer cells usually continue to accumulate new mutations at an accelerated rate, the characteristics of cancer cells within a single case of cancer in a single person may vary markedly, depending on location. This rapid mutability also means that cancers are good at evolving resistance to whatever therapeutic measures are thrown at them.

Of course, many cancers are curable by surgery or radiotherapy if caught at a sufficiently early stage. But, unfortunately, cancers are often caught too late for this satisfying outcome to be feasible. For most adult cancers, once stage IV is reached, the cancer is generally considered to be incurable.

But incurable is not the same as untreatable or uncontrollable. Thanks largely to the rapidly evolving science of molecular biology, cancer scientists are gaining much greater insight. In other words, researchers are learning why many cancers behave the way they do, at a molecular level – how they evade usual mechanisms of growth control, how they evoke the growth of new blood vessels to feed tumor growth, how they migrate through the body and establish new colonies in distant organs, and how they defend themselves from the immune cells that can recognize deviant cells. These new understandings, in turn, are helping cancer scientists to devise new and clever ways that can impede the growth and spread of cancers. These new strategies usually don't amount to cures – only rarely will advanced stage IV cancers be completely eliminated from the body – but they do mean that, in a growing number of patients, it is feasible to manage cancer as a chronic disease – much like diabetes or heart disease – rather than as an inexorable terminal disease.

Oasis of Hope's objective is to use every feasible strategy to achieve cancer control and improve the patient's quality of life. Destroying cancer cells, per se, is no triumph. Helping a patient extend his life and participate in as many normal activities as possible is more important. Of course, treating cancer is a delicate balancing act, because some effective therapies inevitably entail some measure of toxicity and risk. "No pain, no gain," is often as true in cancer therapy as it is in athletics; but at Oasis of Hope, maintaining negative side effects at a bare minimum is a priority.

Oasis of Hope is developing a truly integrative program that incorporates chemotherapy protocols when warranted – but in the context of adjuvant measures that are intended to alleviate side effects while making the therapy more effective for eradicating cancer.

The following pages will describe the integrative regulatory therapy (IRT) protocols currently in use at Oasis of Hope. You will note that a wide range of agents are employed– including a number of nutraceuticals and safe, well-established drugs that are used as adjuvants.

The intent is to use every feasible measure, as supported by clinical data, that may be effective in slowing or reversing cancer spread, while making cancer patients more comfortable and boosting their spirits.

By and large, Oasis of Hope is for patients who wish to collaborate actively with their doctors to do everything rational, feasible, and reasonably safe to keep their cancer at bay and, if possible, reverse it. There are certain limitations to what can be offered at Oasis of Hope. The drugs that are employed are almost always time-tested, and many of them have been around for decades. Often this is an advantage because their potential toxicities are known, and they are usually relatively affordable. Oasis of Hope does not do treatment protocols with experimental new drugs not yet approved for general use. Even if we wanted to do such studies, our patients receive a wide range of nutrients and medications; the combined effects of these adjunctive therapies would likely make it difficult to properly assess the impact of a new medication used concurrently. Also, Oasis of Hope does not have access to some of the hyper-technical cutting-edge strategies in radiotherapy, immunotherapy, or drug delivery that are available at a few specialized research centers. If such measures are potentially beneficial to an Oasis of Hope patient, she is encouraged to incorporate such interventions when feasible. It is common for Oasis of Hope to collaborate with "home physicians" in the management of patients – in other words, some of a patient's therapy is administered at Oasis of Hope, and other therapeutic measures are employed at medical centers closer to the patient's home. In our experience, long-term outcomes are often superior when there is appreciative collaboration between a patient's home physician and those at Oasis of Hope.

Therapy at Oasis of Hope is tailored for the needs of each individual patient. The measures described in this book are all available for use at Oasis of Hope – but whether they are employed in a given patient will hinge on the judgment of that patient's physician and the Oasis of Hope medical team – and of course, the consent of the patient. A team of specialists discusses the patient's case at a biweekly medical board meeting. In this way, each patient benefits from the expertise of a diverse group of physicians, who bring their own unique training and varied experience to the table. It is in these board meetings that a patient's treatment program is customized to address the specific needs of the patient. At each subsequent meeting, the team of doctors looks at new diagnostic information, re-evaluates the patient's case, and makes adjustments as necessary.

Another key feature of therapy at Oasis of Hope is that we take pains to insure that patients have a reasonable understanding of the rationale behind their therapies. Every week, Oasis of Hope patients are encouraged to attend a question-and-answer session at which they can ask staff physicians and medical scientists any questions they might have about their disease or their therapy. There is true give and take at these sessions, and they are sometimes as helpful for the physicians as they are for the patients. Indeed, a few of the therapeutic measures currently included in our protocols came to our attention owing to comments made by patients at these meetings. Dr. Francisco Cecena, who usually presides at these meetings, often encourages our patients to share with us their "cancer wisdom." At Oasis of Hope, patients will find physicians who will really listen to them and do their best to address their concerns.

The science at Oasis of Hope is unique in that there is no disconnect between the research department and the attending physicians. There is a direct connection from the medical literature to the medical practices. This truly is one of the most important factors about Oasis of Hope and greatly responsible for the value of the information presented in the following pages.

Table of Contents

■ ■ ■

1

■ ■ ■

Cancer is a Tough Opponent

Cancer can be – and often is – a very wily opponent. In large measure, this reflects the fact that it is a constantly moving target. To understand why cancers can be so elusive, one must start with how cancers arise.

How Cancers Arise

Throughout life, the human body accumulates mutations in the genetic material of its stem cells – cells that retain the capacity to divide. This genetic material (DNA) can be damaged by activated carcinogens derived from the environment, or by oxidant chemicals produced as a natural part of cellular metabolism. Mutations can also arise when DNA is mis-copied or inappropriately distributed during cellular replication. This is one reason why cancers are most prone to spring up from tissues in which cells have been dividing rapidly. Fortunately, cells have mechanisms for repairing damaged DNA – but these mechanisms are less than perfect, so that permanent alterations of DNA structure are progressively acquired by stem cells. Most of these mutations are either innocuous, having no significant impact on the behavior or survival of the cell, or are deleterious to the cell, dooming it to an early death. But occasionally a mutation arises that is not only tolerated by the cell, but increases the capacity of the cell to survive, proliferate, and migrate. In adult tissues, the total number of cells remains relatively constant owing to a careful balance between cell proliferation and programmed cell death – a process known as "apoptosis."

Tumors develop when this balance is disrupted by mutations that either boost the rate of cellular multiplication, or that protect the aberrant cell from appropriate programmed death. Some of these "oncogenic" (cancer-causing mutations) boost the intensity of growth signals that cause the cell to multiply, or disable key proteins that restrain these growth signals. Others impair the function of proteins that are required for efficient apoptosis. Some mutations, often observed during the early evolution of cancers, increase the propensity of cells to accumulate further mutations. Such mutations typically reduce the cell's capacity to repair damage to its DNA. A loss of the "p53" protein is an example of this. Mutations can increase the probability that dividing cells will end up with too many or too few chromosomes, which is a phenomenon known as "aneuploidy." Pre-cancerous cells – as well as fully evolved cancers – tend to be very genetically labile. In other words, their genetic material mutates faster than that of most healthy cells. Fortunately, a high proportion of stem cells that have acquired potentially oncogenic mutations die off before they can do any harm. That is because many mutations that boost growth signals are somehow "sensed" by the cell as abnormal, inducing the cell to commit suicide. But, this protective apoptotic response can sometimes be "vetoed" if the cell is exposed to excessive levels of certain growth-promoting hormones that suppress apoptosis. Prominent in this regard are sex hormones – estrogen and testosterone – as well as the hormones insulin and insulin-like growth factor-I. The main reason why so-called "Western" cancers – including cancers of the breast, colon, prostate, ovary, and pancreas – have been so much more common in "advanced" societies than in relatively poor Third World cultures is that diets rich in calories, "high-quality" protein and fats, in conjunction with sedentary lifestyles, tend to boost the levels and activities of these cancer-promoting hormones.

Even if incipient cancer cells manage to avoid self-induced apoptosis, they are often vulnerable to attack by marauding "natural killer" immune cells, which can recognize them as the enemy. Sometimes, pre-cancerous cells manage to survive long enough to acquire additional mutations that render them less susceptible to apoptosis or that shield them from attack by natural killer cells. Such cells are prone to give rise to full-blown cancers, which may be relatively difficult to kill with chemotherapy or radiation.

A stem cell, which has acquired mutations that promote its proliferation and survival, may give rise to a tumor. In benign tumors, the cells have not gained the capacity to spread through healthy tissues and establish new distant colonies (metastases). Unless they arise in places where surgery is impractical – certain brain tumors, for example – most benign tumors are little more than a nuisance that can be surgically removed if need be. Some mutated cells gain additional mutations that render them more aggressive, enabling them to spread throughout the body.

A cancer with malignant and metastatic potential must have a remarkable range of capacities. It must produce proteolytic enzymes that enable it to "eat" its way through membranes and healthy tissues, and it must produce "angiogenic" hormones that cause the vascular system to establish a new network of blood vessels to feed the growing tumor. The cancer must gain the ability to invade the blood circulation or lymphatic system to survive while circulating in the blood or lymph, latch on to the wall of small blood vessels or lymphatic ducts, eat its way into new host tissue to establish a metastasis, and evade the natural killer cells that wipe out many incipient metastases before they can establish themselves. It's quite a feat of molecular engineering to accomplish all this, reflecting a delicate balance of multiple acquired mutations. That's why, even though stem cells accumulate many millions of mutations during a lifetime, malignant cancers tend to arise only once or twice over the lifespan. It is frequently feasible to cure localized cancers with surgery or radiotherapy before they acquire the capacity to spread to distant sites. There's no doubt that the most definitive way to truly cure a cancer is to catch it early, before it spreads.

Every Cancer is Unique – and Wily

Cancers arise by progressive accumulation of random mutations. Each cell has tens of thousands of genes, and each of these genes can be altered in literally hundreds of ways. So each cancer is absolutely unique. Moreover, because cancers tend to acquire mutations more rapidly than healthy cells, they are constantly evolving – the cells within a given tumor are often diverse, and a cancer tends to evolve over the course of time. This evolution is often directed by the stresses that the cancer is subjected to. For example, when a cancer is assaulted with a cytotoxic chemotherapy drug, the few cells in the tumor that have acquired mutations that enable them to detoxify or expel this drug, or that otherwise render them relatively resistant to the toxicity of the drug, are prone to survive. These cells will then predominate when the tumor grows back following chemotherapy. The result is a tumor that will be less responsive to that particular drug – and possibly other drugs as well – the next time that chemotherapy is attempted. Analogously, if a cancer is treated with anti-angiogenic agents that impair its ability to elicit the growth of new blood vessels, cancer cells which mutate in a way that boosts their ability to produce pro-angiogenic factors may be able to continue spreading and promoting renewed tumor growth. Cancers can also mutate in ways that render them relatively resistant to killing by natural killer cells, which makes it more difficult to eradicate small tumors with immunotherapy. Cancer is in fact a formidable adversary.

Although each cancer is unique, there is a tendency for cancers which arise from a given tissue to have certain common properties. For example, clinical experience teaches that initially certain types of cancer tend to be susceptible to destruction with a specific cytotoxic drug, or perhaps radiotherapy. Moreover, certain specific types of mutations tend to be highly common in certain types of tumors. This can have implications for the measures that may be effective for controlling the growth, or exterminating, that type of cancer. Well-trained oncologists aren't just flying blind. They can make educated, and often accurate, guesses regarding the therapeutic strategies that are likely to be useful in a given type of cancer. But, because every cancer is truly unique, there is never one-hundred-percent certainty that a given therapy will be effective – and, because cancers are constantly evolving, a therapy that formerly was highly effective may prove to be considerably less so when it is attempted again.

2
■ ■ ■

Oasis of Hope Integrative Regulatory Therapies: A Multi-Focal Strategy for Cancer Control

Cancer is heavy-handed. There is nothing subtle at all about the presence of a malignant tumor in the kidney or lung. Cancer makes no attempt to veil its threat. It is a disease that can gather momentum quickly and attack with frightening ferocity. Only a concerted and combined effort can repel such an attack. Dr. Contreras, Sr. believed that to defeat cancer, it was necessary to attack it from every possible angle. He understood the importance of both direct and indirect approaches. The foundation of the Metabolic Therapy that he devised is its multi-faceted approach. Yes, we do attack the tumor, but we also stimulate the immune system, shield normal healthy tissues from the attack, and address causal factors.

The total care approach requires the patient's full participation. Cancer treatment is not a spectator sport. The patient must be prepared for the fight. We go through a process of structuring a patient for success by providing the necessary resources to face the threat at the physical, emotional, and spiritual levels. There is no question that the alliance between body, mind, and spirit can even the playing field against cancer. In the chapters that follow, the Oasis of Hope body/mind/spirit medicine therapeutic protocols will be explained. The present chapter constitutes an overview that will explain how Oasis of Hope attacks cancer, sensitizes it to this attack, cuts off its supply lines, and blocks its avenues of spread.

It is probably unrealistic to expect that the "wonder drug" for "curing" cancer is just about to emerge from some pharmaceutical lab. Cancer is so wily that the chance that it will remain permanently responsive to any single agent is quite low. That's why an integrative cancer therapy approach, that intervenes simultaneously in as many ways as is feasible to promote the death and impede the spread of cancer cells, is likely to remain the most effective and logical way to control cancers that are no longer localized.

In addition, it is important to remember that the ultimate goal when treating advanced cancer is to insure that patients can enjoy a reasonably high quality of life during the months and years that they are managing cancer. All too often, traditional oncologists are so focused on the tumor that they show insufficient regard for the overall psychological and physical health of their patients. Truly compassionate cancer therapy should address the psychological and spiritual well being of cancer patients as a way of helping them to maintain a hopeful, and reasonably cheerful, attitude even if the chance of definitive "cure" must realistically be viewed as small. After all, mortality is a reality that most well adjusted people learn to cope with while enjoying life and being grateful for the time on Earth that they are allotted. There is no reason why the attitude of cancer patients, even those with advanced disease, should be any different – provided that appropriate measures are taken to minimize the pain and disability that often accompany cancer and cancer therapy. So the purpose of integrative cancer therapy should be, not just to maximize survival, but also to maximize the number of months and, hopefully, years of high-quality life that the patient can enjoy.

Now that an overview of the nature of cancer and of the fundamental goals that underlie the Oasis of Hope approach to cancer therapy has been presented, a closer look at the strategies that Oasis of Hope employs in its Integrative Regulatory Therapies (IRT) for cancer will follow.

The Oasis of Hope IRT Protocols

Patients at Oasis of Hope are enrolled into one of two main protocols, known as "IRT-Q" and "IRT-C." Although these protocols share many common features, they are differentiated by the fact that patients on the IRT-Q protocol receive cytotoxic chemotherapy, whereas those on the IRT-C protocol do not, but rather receive extra infusions of high-dose intravenous vitamin C as an alternative approach to attacking the cancer. Patients on each protocol receive a range of additional interventions including oxidative preconditioning therapy, redox regulatory therapy, cell signal transduction modulatory therapy, metronomic chemotherapy, cancer-retarding anti-inflammatory therapies, optimal diet and exercise, and emotional and spiritual support. This may sound very complicated, but in the following pages, the why and how of each of these approaches will be explained.

Destroying Cancer Cells with Chemotherapy – the IRT-Q Protocol

For some types of advanced cancer, specific cytotoxic chemotherapy drugs are known to have at least some efficacy in a high proportion of cases – especially if the patient has not received that drug previously. For patients who fall into this category, and whose physical condition makes chemotherapy feasible, Oasis of Hope physicians will usually recommend an IRT-Q protocol. The "Q" reflects the fact that the Spanish word for "chemotherapy" is "quimioterapia." Patients enrolled in an IRT-Q protocol will visit the clinic at least three times for a course of appropriate chemotherapy. The chemotherapy regimens employed at Oasis of Hope are well documented in the medical literature, and are used in the full doses shown to have potential efficacy.

What sets Oasis of Hope apart from many other clinics employing chemotherapy is its use of many adjuvant measures intended to make the chemotherapy more effective at annihilating cancer cells, while simultaneously minimizing the damage done to healthy tissues. These measures are cited very briefly here. Later in the book, a more detailed explanation of these measures, with citations of the relevant biomedical literature, will be provided.

Coping with Tumor Hypoxia

One way to make chemotherapy more effective is to insure that cancer cells are adequately oxygenated. Because tumors tend to have haphazard blood supplies, some parts of tumors tend to receive relatively little blood flow, and are thus poorly oxygenated (hypoxic). For reasons that are not yet entirely clear, hypoxic cancer cells are often harder to kill with chemotherapy. So we use several strategies for improving the oxygenation of tumors. Prior to the administration of chemotherapy, patients are infused intravenously with a perfluorocarbon polymer called "Perftec." This is an oxygen carrier that complements the ability of red blood cells to deliver oxygen to the tumor. Because the particles of Perftec are so much smaller than red blood cells, they can flow through constricted capillaries that would exclude red blood cells. The oxygen-carrying capacity of Perftec is boosted by having the patients breathe oxygen-enriched air when chemotherapy drugs are subsequently administered. Another way in which we improve tumor oxygenation is by administering ozone autohemotherapy prior to chemotherapy. This strategy has been shown to make red blood cells more flexible and blood less viscous, thereby boosting blood flow through hypoxic tumor regions. Ozone autohemotherapy also increases the capacity of red blood cells to deliver oxygen to the tumor.

Oasis of Hope has also developed a novel strategy for increasing the chemosensitivity of cancer cells that nevertheless remain hypoxic. Recent research demonstrates that hypoxia protects tumor cells, at least in part, by diminishing the capacity of these cells to produce an intracellular signaling factor known as cyclic GMP (cGMP). Prior to chemotherapy, Oasis of Hope administers high oral doses of the B-vitamin biotin. In high concentrations, biotin has been shown to directly stimulate cGMP production, both in tumors and healthy tissues. Fortunately, increased cGMP doesn't seem to influence the chemosensitivity of cells that are well oxygenated, so biotin shouldn't boost the chemosensitivity of healthy tissues.

Chemosensitizing Agents

Recent rodent research shows that high but tolerable intakes of the antioxidant nutrient selenium can boost the chemosensitivity of many types of cancer while making healthy tissues more chemoresistant. With this rationale, Oasis of Hope employs high-dose selenium supplementation prior to and during chemotherapy. Another agent, which boosts the chemosensitivity of many cancers is the activated metabolite of vitamin D (calcitriol). Since some cancers are capable of making their own calcitriol when supplied with vitamin D, we use high but safe doses of that vitamin in conjunction with chemotherapy.

In many cancers, their relative chemoresistance reflects increased intracellular activity of a factor known as NF-kappaB. Since the natural drug salicylate and the herbal compound silibinin have shown the capacity to inhibit NF-kappaB activity in clinically feasible doses, these agents are also employed as chemosensitizing agents in the IRT-Q protocols.

Other agents which have potential for chemosensitizing certain tumors, and that are often administered in conjunction with chemotherapy at Oasis of Hope include boswellic acids (derived from an Ayurvedic herbal preparation with anti-inflammatory activity), and the drugs pioglitazone, diclofenac, and valproic acid. Suffice it to say that we spare little effort to insure that the chemotherapy we employ will kill as many cancer cells as is physically possible.

Protecting Healthy Tissues

One reason why the IRT-Q protocols are gaining increased popularity with our patients is that we incorporate several measures to protect healthy tissues, which makes chemotherapy a less traumatic experience. The ozone autohemotherapy mentioned above has a dual purpose – in addition to improving tumor oxygenation, it also provides oxidative pre-conditioning. The chemically altered compounds in ozonated blood are "perceived" by healthy tissues as a sign of oxidative stress. In response, these tissues boost their production of antioxidant enzymes and other protective factors. Then, when chemotherapy is subsequently administered, these tissues are better able to cope with the pro-oxidant activity of these cytotoxic drugs, so that they are less damaged. This translates into less bone marrow damage, less nausea, and fewer side effects of other kinds.

As noted, the high-dose selenium employed with IRT-Q has the potential to protect normal tissues. Another component of IRT-Q that is protective in this regard is the hormone melatonin, which mitigates chemotherapy-induced damage of the bone marrow. In addition, supplementation with the amino acid glutamine, a key source of calories for cells in the intestinal tract, is employed to reduce damage to these cells.

Quite commonly, patients comment on how much better they tolerated chemotherapy at Oasis of Hope compared with prior negative experiences with chemotherapy at other clinics. This, despite the fact that Oasis of Hope physicians don't hold back when it comes to dosing. The increase in efficacy, coupled with the decrease in negative side effects, reflects thoughtful planning.

An Alternative Strategy for Eliminating Cancer-IRT-C

Some types of cancer are not very responsive to available chemotherapeutic drugs. Some patients may have clinical conditions, such as bone marrow depression or bile duct blockage that make chemotherapy inadvisable. On occasion, some patients simply refuse to accept chemotherapy, owing to negative past experiences with it in their own lives or that of a loved one. For patients who fall into these categories, Oasis of Hope offers an alternative protocol known as IRT-C. The intent of this strategy is to induce oxidative stress in the tumors by employing intravenous infusion of sodium ascorbate (a form of vitamin C) and Vitamin K3 (menadione) to generate hydrogen peroxide in the tumor. For the many cancers that are relatively deficient in the antioxidant enzyme catalase, this approach has the potential to kill cancer cells selectively while healthy cells remain unharmed. We have found that some patients show a very gratifying response to this strategy. In patients whose tumors are potentially responsive to chemotherapy but whose physical condition is not yet ready to tolerate it, IRT-C often provides enough tumor control to give their normal tissues a chance to heal, so that they again become appropriate candidates for chemotherapy.

It stands to reason that hypoxic tumor cells are likely to be less responsive to intravenous ascorbate, owing to the fact that ascorbate must react with molecular oxygen to generate the hydrogen peroxide that can be toxic to the tumor. To combat tumor hypoxia, Perftec and ozonated autohemotherapy are included in the IRT-C protocol, as well as the chemosensitizing agents employed with IRT-Q.

3
∎ ∎ ∎

Oasis of Hope At - Home Therapies

With most chemotherapies, it is necessary to give the body at least a few weeks to heal before another course of chemotherapy is administered. This is why Oasis of Hope patients go home for several weeks in between courses of chemotherapy. Oasis of Hope provides its patients with an elaborate at-home therapeutic regimen with the intent of slowing the grow-back of remaining tumors between sessions of chemotherapy. The rate of tumor grow-back between cycles of chemotherapy can have an important impact on the chances for a curative outcome, or at least for significant tumor control. If the tumor grows back so rapidly that the number of malignant cells eliminated by a course of chemotherapy is entirely replaced by the growing tumor before another round of therapy can be administered, the at-home strategy will at best temporarily keep the tumor in check. On the other hand, chemotherapy may have a chance to induce a substantial remission if each course kills a significant number of cells, and grow-back between chemo sessions is slow.

Patients in the IRT-C protocol also return home for several weeks between their courses of ascorbate infusions. They receive the same At-Home therapeutic regimen as patients receiving IRT-Q. The rationale of the At-Home therapy in IRT-C is the same − to slow the grow-back of tumor between sessions of in-hospital vitamin C infusions.

The therapeutic strategies described here are also employed in the long-term follow-up (or maintenance) therapy prescribed for Oasis of Hope patients after they have completed an IRT-Q or IRT-C protocol.

The intent here is to slow the growth of residual tumor, postponing as long as possible the need for further cytotoxic therapies.

The tumor-retardant strategies employed in the Oasis of Hope At-Home regimens have several goals:

• To slow tumor growth by intervening directly in signaling pathways that make cancer grow more rapidly and aggressively;
• To inhibit the angiogenic process that makes tumor spread possible by providing new blood vessels for the tumor;
• To boost the capacity of natural killer cells to eliminate new small metastases or residual nests of cancer cells;
• To decrease risk for new metastases by intervening in the metastatic process;
• To minimize risk for cachexia, a common "paraneoplastic" complication of tumor spread, entailing substantial loss of muscle mass.

Slowing Tumor Growth

One way in which we strive to suppress tumor growth is by decreasing blood levels of certain pro-growth hormones, such as insulin, free IGF-I, and free estrogen, that promote increased growth and survival of many types of cancer cells. This is achieved with a lifestyle program that stresses a low fat, whole-food vegan or quasi-vegan diet, a regular program of aerobic exercise training, such as brisk walking, and a reduction of excess body fat in overweight patients fighting cancers in which obesity has a known negative prognostic impact.

A number of nutraceuticals and drugs employed in the Oasis of Hope At-Home regimens have the potential to act directly on many tumors to slow tumor growth. These include: salicylic acid (salsalate), silibinin, diclofenac (an inexpensive cox-2 inhibitor), boswellic acids, pioglitazone, vitamin D, valproic acid, and soy isoflavones in prostate, colon, and ovarian cancers.

Suppressing Angiogenesis

A key strategy that Oasis of Hope uses to impede the angiogenic process is called "metronomic chemotherapy." This entails the daily use of one or more chemotherapy drugs in a dose so low that no significant toxicity to healthy tissues or side effects result. Remarkably, such chemotherapy has been shown to be selectively toxic to endothelial cells that are engaged in building new blood vessels for the tumor. There is reason to believe that the anti-diabetes drug pioglitazone, included in the At-Home regimens, will further boost the sensitivity of endothelial cells to metronomic chemotherapy.

Other nutraceuticals and drugs employed in the At-Home regimens with potential for slowing angiogenesis include: The chief compound in green tea polyphenols (EGCG), the amino acid glycine, salsalate, silibinin, diclofenac, valproic acid, vitamin D, and fish oil.

Supporting the Immune Attack on Cancer - Boosting Natural Killer Cell Function

The At-Home regimen includes a number of agents that can aid the immune system's ability to attack cancer by boosting the function of natural killer cells. One of the most intriguing is the hormone melatonin, administered once daily before bedtime. Multiple clinical studies in Italy show that this regimen tends to have a very favorable, statistically significant impact on survival in cancer patients. This favorable impact of melatonin on natural killer cell function seems likely to be the chief mediator of this benefit. Other agents with likely benefit in this regard employed by Oasis of Hope include selenium, diclofenac, valproic acid, and glutamine. Moreover, there is recent evidence that metronomic chemotherapy has a favorable impact on the capacity of natural killer cells to attack cancer cells as it selectively eliminates a type of white cell called a "T-Reg" cell that suppresses the cytotoxic activity of natural killer cells.

Preventing Metastases

The At-Home regimens include one agent that specifically targets the metastatic process – modified citrus pectin derived from the chief form of fiber in citrus fruits. This absorbable form of pectin interacts with galectin-3, a type of molecular "hook" that cancer cells, when circulating in the bloodstream, use to attach themselves to the walls of small blood vessels (capillaries). This sort of attachment is required before cancer cells can migrate through the capillary wall to establish a new metastasis. Modified citrus pectin suppresses this process by blocking the grasping function of galectin-3.

Preventing Cachexia

A substantial loss of muscle mass (cachexia) is a common complication of advanced cancer. Although loss of appetite associated with decreased calorie consumption is typically seen with this syndrome, the substantial loss of muscle mass associated with cachexia reflects an inflammatory reaction in skeletal muscle fibers that is much more severe than that loss of muscle mass seen with caloric restriction alone. In some patients, this loss of muscle mass becomes so severe that it contributes to death by severely weakening the respiratory muscles. The Oasis of Hope At-Home regimen includes several elements that have potential for preventing cachexia, including salsalate, melatonin, glutamate, and fish oil.

Supporting The Whole Person

Oasis of Hope was one of the first cancer clinics to include music, laughter, and art therapies as options for its patients. The hospital features a lovely non-denominational chapel and prayer partners to whom patients have ready access. Spiritually- themed lectures stressing hope and compassion are often presented at Oasis of Hope. Patients are encouraged to wear regular clothes instead of hospital gowns, to eat together in the communal dining hall where three delicious quasi-vegan meals are served each day, and to develop friendships and share experiences with their fellow patients. Frequent communication between doctors and patients is also encouraged. Every week there is a question-and-answer session in which several physicians strive to answer any question that the patients care to ask about their therapy. The sincerely respectful relationship between patients and caregivers at Oasis of Hope – a contrast to the rather perfunctory attention from doctors that patients often receive at more traditional cancer clinics – undoubtedly contributes to the more positive, hopeful attitude which patients often develop during their association with us. No doubt the hopeful atmosphere is aided by the fact that, as patients can readily see, the clinic staff work hard to help them in any way feasible. These efforts frequently translate into excellent clinical results.

Alteration of Lifestyle

While patients receive treatment at Oasis of Hope, we begin to educate them on how to live healthy lives when they return home and how to continue therapy. Oasis of Hope doctors and nurses work with patients and their loved ones to teach them how to effectively self-administer therapies. This is a very cost-effective way for patients to continue therapy for a prolonged period of time.

Doctors at Oasis of Hope Hospital have observed that the patients who get the best results are those who make a real commitment to the program, the ones who have the discipline and desire to adhere to the therapies prescribed. A tragic error that many patients make is to abandon therapy as soon as they start to feel better or when they experience remission. Those who continue therapy, adhere to the nutrition program, and come back for the maintenance treatments and the follow-up program, gain the best results.

This is why the hospital's administration developed a program for patients to come back every six months for two-day follow-up visits, with their doctors at no charge. The follow-up program lasts a full five years at no additional cost to the patient. At these follow-up visits, all the doctors monitor the patient's progress and make any modifications to the home care therapy that will better meet the patient's healthcare needs. We believe that the periodic phone calls we make to the patients have been vital because people need the encouragement and need to know that their doctor really cares.

Every patient is encouraged to completely adhere to the therapies and embrace the lifestyle changes recommended at Oasis of Hope. A patient's commitment to the therapy is the single most important factor that determines how effective treatment is. That is why this final component of the Oasis of Hope medical treatment program is just as vital as the others.

4
• • •

The Oasis of Hope Difference

The therapy regimens offered by Oasis of Hope are distinguished by the fact that they are:

Personalized – Although the IRT-Q and IRT-C regimens are rather well defined, they are personalized in line with the particular needs of each patient. The choice of the chemotherapy drug employed will depend upon the type of cancer, the stage of its spread, and the physical condition of the patient. The adjuvant regimen can be modified as needed to insure that that it is well tolerated by the patient, and that it is the most appropriate regimen for the tumor type. Patients who prefer to avoid cytotoxic chemotherapy drugs can be treated with the IRT-C protocol. Oasis of Hope doctors do their best to inform patients of the potential benefits and risks associated with the therapeutic protocols which they recommend – and it is ultimately the patient who decides whether a recommended protocol is implemented.

Integral and Integrative – As should be clear from the foregoing discussion, no effort is spared to maximize both the efficacy and the tolerability of therapy regimens. The focus is on a diverse array of targets and the utilization of a wide range of available nutraceuticals and safe drugs. This is done within the context of a program that strives to optimize the psychological and overall physical status of the patient, with the intent of maximizing good quality survival. That's why Oasis of Hope therapies are regarded as "integral" since they integrate a broad range of measures and goals. This strategy may also be characterized as integrative, since it strives to combine, in a logical fashion, the most credible and effective resources of "conventional" and "alternative" medicine.

Permanent – A patient's relationship with Oasis of Hope is intended to be permanent. After a total course of IRT-Q or IRT-C is completed, patients return home with an elaborate maintenance regimen intended to control the growth of any remaining tumor cells. Patients are encouraged to return on a regular basis for follow-up evaluations, which may result in further therapy courses when advisable. The intent of therapy, at least in patients who can't be completely cured, is to turn cancer into a chronic disease that can be managed on a long-term basis, much like diabetes or hypertension are treated. An effort is made to aid patients maintain a high-quality lifestyle while coping with their disorders. Therapy protocols at Oasis of Hope are constantly being up-dated, to keep pace with the latest developments in cancer research. Occasionally, on follow-up visits, patients may have access to new therapeutic options that weren't available during their previous visits. These follow-up visits can also be helpful to other Oasis of Hope patients, since it can be inspiring and encouraging for them to meet with "veteran" Oasis of Hope patients who have achieved cancer control and a good quality of life. The patients have the comfort of knowing that their caregivers at Oasis of Hope are part of their "team" for life – and that they themselves are valued partners in this team.

Dynamic – The medical scientists who devise the IRT-Q and IRT-C regimens are constantly scanning the latest credible biomedical literature to enhance their understanding of cancer and to improve the efficacy and scope of the Oasis of Hope therapy regimens. That means that these regimens are in a constant state of revision and new agents, or improved forms or dosages of agents already in use, are frequently incorporated into them. Oasis of Hope strives to define the cutting edge of integrative cancer treatment.

Supporting Patients in Every Way

The logical rationale for virtually every element incorporated into Oasis of Hope treatment protocols is supported by data published in hundreds of medical journal articles. Every effort is made to use nutraceuticals and drugs that are safe, relatively well tolerated, and reasonably affordable when compared with newly-approved cancer drugs, which may cost many thousands of dollars per month. Most of the patients at Oasis of Hope are there because they have already been through traditional medical therapies, which, despite the best-intentioned efforts of their doctors, ultimately failed to provide an adequate measure of cancer control. For these patients, Oasis of Hope can indeed be the "oasis of hope" that its name implies. We use our best judgment, based on diligent study of the medical literature, to develop therapy regimens that incorporate the most recent and promising findings. Our commitment is to continuously improve and update our therapies in line with the most recent clinical data published.

5

. . .

Oxidizing Cancer to Death

Oxidant Stress – and How Cells Cope with It

It is common knowledge that "free radicals" and "oxidants" are important mediators of disease – but what are these compounds? In most stable molecules, electrons occur in pairs. Molecules that contain unpaired electrons tend to be unstable and are known as "radicals" or "free radicals." Because they are unstable, they have a tendency to extract another electron from another molecule, or to donate their unpaired electron to another molecule. In either case, the attacked molecule is usually converted to a radical in the process. In living cells, this can give rise to a chain reaction of molecular damage.

The chief way in which free radicals arise in a body's cells is by donation of an electron to molecular oxygen, generating a compound known as superoxide. This reaction can be catalyzed by several natural enzymatic reactions in cells. Superoxide can then, via spontaneous or enzyme-catalyzed reactions, give rise to other reactive compounds such as hydrogen peroxide or peroxynitrite. These compounds are not themselves free radicals, but they often give rise to free radicals, and they also can act to alter the structure and function of proteins by "oxidizing" them. Unsaturated fatty acids in membranes are also prone to oxidation by free radicals.

Because unabated damage by free radicals and oxidants can cause major and often adverse changes in the structures of cellular proteins and fats, living organisms have developed antioxidant mechanisms.

Certain enzymes, as well as electron-donor molecules known as antioxidants, can "fix" free radicals by electron donation.

This can work in other ways to prevent or undo the damage to biological molecules wrought by oxidant reactions. Examples include enzymes such as superoxide dismutase, catalase, glutathione peroxidase, and thioreductase, and antioxidant molecules such as glutathione and vitamins C and E. In normal healthy cellular metabolism, the production of oxidants is balanced by the action of antioxidant mechanisms that prevent free radical damage from getting out of hand and overwhelming the cell. But sometimes, either because of excess production of radicals and oxidants, or because of inadequately protective antioxidant mechanisms, free radical damage can get the upper hand – a condition known as "oxidant stress." Oxidant stress is not always bad. In fact, induction of oxidant stress is one way in which some cytotoxic drugs kill cancer cells. On the other hand, as we shall see, a constant moderate level of oxidant stress in some cancers renders them more aggressive and harder to kill.

A high proportion of cancers have low activity of the enzyme catalase, which degrades the oxidant chemical hydrogen peroxide[1-3]. This adaptation may be beneficial to the cancer. Although oxidant chemicals can be toxic to cells, moderate increases in oxidant stress aid the growth and survival of many cancers[4-7]. However, low catalase makes cancers potentially vulnerable to attack with hydrogen peroxide. Recently, researchers at the National Institutes of Health have discovered that high concentrations of vitamin C (ascorbate) can react spontaneously with molecular oxygen within tumors to generate large amounts of hydrogen peroxide, which can be lethal to tumor cells whose catalase activity is low[8,9].

Such large concentrations can only be achieved by high dose intravenous infusions of vitamin C. Oral administration is ineffective in this regard [10]. These findings rationalize several previous case reports of objective tumor regression in cancer patients treated repeatedly with high-dose intravenous vitamin C [11-13].

Vitamin C is not toxic to normal healthy tissues because they have ample amounts of catalase activity. The current protocol insures that blood and tissue levels of vitamin C will remain high, with millimolar levels close to those of blood sugar for at least 4 hours.

Vitamin K3 as an Adjuvant

The ability of ascorbate (vitamin C) to generate hydrogen peroxide in tumors apparently hinges on the presence of unknown catalysts that can transfer electrons from ascorbate to oxygen molecules, generating the unstable compound superoxide[8,9]. The latter is rapidly converted to hydrogen peroxide, which can move into cancer cells, and mediates the tumor cell death achieved with successful ascorbate therapy. Dr. Mark Levine, whose research encouraged us to develop the IRT-C protocol, speculates that extracellular protein-bound iron serves as this catalyst[9]. It is conceivable that the availability of this catalyst might vary from tissue to tissue and person to person, depending on nutritional status or genetics. Furthermore, there is no reason to assume that levels of this catalyst are sufficient to permit an optimally intense generation of hydrogen peroxide in tissues.

However, it is not necessary to rely on unknown endogenous catalysts for this purpose. Certain small soluble organic molecules can perform the same catalytic function, expediting the transfer of electrons from ascorbate to oxygen. In particular, menadione, also known as vitamin K3, has this capacity[14]. Menadione may be particularly appropriate for this purpose, as it has long been in clinical use as a source of vitamin K activity [15].

Moreover, there is substantial research literature demonstrating that joint incubation with sodium ascorbate and menadione is often selectively toxic to cancer cells. This phenomenon has been demonstrated with a wide range of human and rodent cancer [16-20]. In striking parallel to the studies which report that high concentrations of ascorbate alone can exert such toxicity, it has been shown that concurrent incubation with the enzyme catalase – which destroys hydrogen peroxide – markedly alleviates this toxicity, demonstrating that hydrogen peroxide mediates this cancer-killing effect.

Furthermore, cancer cells which express relatively low levels of catalase are more susceptible to this toxicity than cancer cells with higher levels of this activity. The selective susceptibility of cancer cells, as contrasted to normal cells, reflects the tendency of cancers to have lower levels of catalase and other enzymes which dispose of hydrogen peroxide[14,21]. This, in turn, may reflect the fact that low concentrations of hydrogen peroxide promote cellular proliferation and survival in many cancers. In other words, low catalase activity, by enabling cancers to sustain modest concentrations of hydrogen peroxide, may make some cancers more aggressive and viable[21] – that is, until they are assaulted with high concentrations of ascorbate.

Researchers at the Catholic University of Louvain, Belgium, have played a pioneering role in demonstrating the potential utility of ascorbate/menadione in cancer therapy. In particular, they have shown that injection, or even oral administration of these agents, can retard cancer growth and metastasis in tumor-bearing rodents[14,22,23]. They report that this therapy is well tolerated, without any evident damage to healthy tissues, and they recommend that this strategy should be assessed in clinical trials.

They also demonstrate that ascorbate/menadione can interact synergistically with certain cytotoxic chemotherapy drugs in killing cancer cells, presumably because a concurrent increase in oxidant stress can make these drugs more lethal [24]. This observation has been independently confirmed[25]. Indeed, there are reports that menadione alone can potentiate the cytotoxicity of certain chemotherapy agents, presumably because, in sufficiently high concentrations, intracellular menadione can generate oxidant stress by transferring electrons from intracellular molecules to oxygen[26,27]. Injectible vitamin K3 is administered, just prior to the vitamin C infusions, with the hope and expectation that inclusion of menadione in the ascorbate infusions will markedly potentiate a generation of hydrogen peroxide in tumors, enabling a more substantial cell kill in those cancers that are sufficiently low in catalase activity.

Tumor Oxygenation – Ozone and Perftec

However, this strategy can only work well in tumors that have adequate levels of oxygen, as ascorbate reacts with oxygen to produce the hydrogen peroxide. Portions of many tumors tend to be hypoxic, as the blood flow through tumors is often sluggish compared to that which supplies normal tissues. This evidently could compromise the anti-tumor efficacy of vitamin C therapy.

To overcome this problem, Oasis of Hope Hospital employs several complementary techniques that can boost the oxygen content of tumors. Ozone autohemotherapy (O3-AHT) alters the properties of blood so that it is less viscous, its cellular elements are more flexible, and its oxygenated red blood cells surrender oxygen to tissues more readily. This is shown as a rightward shift of dissociation curve. It also promotes vasodilation by stimulating nitric oxide release by the endothelial lining of small arteries [28].

The net result is more oxygen delivery to the tumor [29,30]. Many tumors contain regions in which oxygen content is low, and hypoxic tumor cells typically are harder to kill with radiotherapy or chemotherapy. Thus, protocols which can boost tumor oxygen levels have potential as adjuvant measures in cancer therapy. Recently, researchers at the Canary Islands Institute for Cancer Research recruited 18 cancer patients and used special needle probes to measure the oxygen content of their tumors before and after 3 sessions of O3-AHT. They were in fact able to establish that there were fewer hypoxic tumor regions following O3-AHT [29].

At Oasis of Hope, O3-AHT is used not only in conjunction with chemotherapy, but also with high-dose intravenous sodium ascorbate therapy for IRT-C. This strategy involves drawing 200 ml. of a patient's blood, treating it with a mixture of ozone and oxygen, and re-infusing it.

This procedure is typically repeated several times weekly. It is important to stress that Oasis of Hope employs an O3-AHT protocol that has been widely utilized in Europe for decades with an excellent safety record. The safety of this strategy reflects the fact that no ozone is infused into the body. Ozone is very unstable, and for practical purposes is completely dissipated before the ozone-treated blood is returned to the body. Thus, the body is exposed to ozone oxidation products, rather than ozone itself. Exposure of blood to ozone in clinically appropriate amounts does not cause lysis of red blood cells, or compromise the functional viability of white cells. No evident side effects are noted in patients receiving O3-AHT.

Oasis of Hope also has a novel perfluorochemical emulsion known as Perftec that is an oxygen carrier. When infused into a patient, it greatly boosts the total oxygen carrying capacity of blood[31]. After Perftec infusion, patients are asked to breathe air that is enriched in oxygen content, so that the circulating Perftec is loaded with optimal amounts of oxygen.

The combination of ozone autohemotherapy and Perftec infusion can be expected to improve oxygen availability in hypoxic regions of tumors. This in turn should boost the ability of intravenous ascorbate and vitamin K to generate hydrogen peroxide in tumors.

Concurrent Chemotherapy

Many patients will also receive cancer chemotherapy on the same day that they receive intravenous vitamin C. There are reasons to believe that the oxidant stress induced by the vitamin C in the tumor, as well as the improved tumor oxygenation made possible by ozone therapy and Perftec, will often increase the ability of the administered chemotherapy drugs to kill cancer cells [32-38]. The Oasis of Hope Vitamin C Protocol has been designed to exploit these complementary interactions so that destruction of cancer cells can be maximized without increasing the toxic risk to healthy tissues.

Although many patients will be treated with chemotherapy, some will not. In some cases, the type of cancer is known to be resistant to available chemotherapy drugs. In other cases, patients elect to forego chemotherapy for personal reasons. For these patients, it is hoped that a vitamin C & K3/tumor oxygenation regimen will be sufficient to achieve worthwhile destruction of the tumor.

Other Adjuvant Measures

We are currently employing additional adjuvant measures that, in at least some tumors, are likely to potentiate the killing of tumor cells achieved through our vitamin C & K3/chemotherapy regimen. The natural compound salicylate is derived from white willow bark, which has been used for centuries as an anti-inflammatory therapy. It can enhance the sensitivity of many tumors to chemotherapy and hydrogen peroxide by inhibiting the activity of "NF-kappaB" [39,40]. This factor is activated in a high proportion of advanced cancers, and works in multiple ways to render these cancers less sensitive to chemotherapy and oxidant stress [41,42]. Although the drug aspirin is a chemical relative of salicylate, the latter does not have the potential to cause bleeding ulcers or kidney failure as aspirin does [43,44]. The main common side effect of salicylic acid therapy is a reversible impairment of ear function associated with a mild loss of hearing acuity and/ or "ringing in the ears" (tinnitus). These problems go away after salicylate is discontinued [45]. At Oasis of Hope Hospital, the form of salicylate we use is known as "salsalate' (Disalcid). This is less likely to cause stomach upset than is sodium salicylate [46].

Prior to receiving vitamin K3 and vitamin C (and possibly chemotherapy), patients are also supplemented with the nutrient selenium and the herb silymarin, which is a source of the natural anti-inflammatory compound silibinin.

Like salicylate, these agents have potential for sensitizing tumors to destruction by chemotherapy or oxidant stress. Silymarin's activity in this regard may be similar to salicylate's. It suppresses activation of NF-kappaB [47,48]. Recent studies show that high doses of organic selenium can make cancer cells more sensitive to many types of chemotherapeutic drugs [49]. There are reasons to believe that selenium may also make hydrogen peroxide more lethal to tumors. We now administer selenium in a form known as methylselenocysteine (MSC), which is a natural organic form found in certain foods. MSC is the preferable form for this application because it is rapidly metabolized to release the organic selenium metabolites useful in cancer therapy. We also will be exploring the use of activated vitamin D (calcitriol) as a chemosensitizing agent in cancer therapy.

Calcitriol appears to be quite safe if administered in only one or two doses a week, and if the concurrent diet is relatively low in calcium [50]. Calcitriol has been shown to boost the sensitivity of many cancers to chemotherapy drugs or hydrogen peroxide [51,52]. During their stay at Oasis of Hope Hospital, patients will also be supplemented with various nutrients such as fish oil, green tea polyphenols, and melatonin. The purpose is to slow tumor growth by blocking new blood vessel formation (angiogenesis) or boosting the body's immune capacities. Supplementation with these nutrients will continue after patients return home between hospital therapy sessions. This "after-therapy" can be crucial for improving chances of a cure or at least achieving a worthwhile prolongation of high-quality life.

Don't Be Confused

Controlled clinical studies that show that "vitamin C therapy" does not work in cancer only assessed oral vitamin C therapy [11]. As noted, oral vitamin C can achieve only very modest increases in blood ascorbate levels. Intravenous vitamin C therapy has far greater credibility, and indeed is currently being formally evaluated in clinical trials at the U.S. National Institutes of Health.

6
. . .

Modulating Cellular Signal Transduction

Over the last several decades, molecular biology has gradually been unraveling the way in which the body's cells work. "Signal transduction" refers to the way in which cellular proteins undergo small and usually reversible alterations in their structure to induce alterations in cell behavior. For example, the catalytic activities of many enzymes are altered through a process known as "phosphorylation." In this process, phosphate groups are attached to specific amino acids – usually serine or tyrosine. The enzymes which attach phosphate groups to proteins are known as "kinases." Their activity is opposed by another group of enzymes, "phosphatases," which remove phosphate groups from proteins. Oftentimes, kinases and phosphatases are themselves susceptible to phosphorylations that change their activities [1]. Another common way in which the functional properties of cellular proteins are altered is by "oxidation." Oxidant stress can lead to the production of hydrogen peroxide, which can interact with certain cysteine amino acids in proteins to change their functional properties [2,3]. These alterations can be reversed by another group of enzymes known as "reductases."

These considerations may sound very abstruse to someone who hasn't had a chance to study molecular biology, but they have very practical implications for the way cells behave. For example, hormones which bind to cellular receptors often induce these receptors to undergo self-induced phosphorylations of tyrosines in these receptors.

This in turn sets off a chain reaction of alterations in the structures of many proteins that can trigger cellular multiplication or migration, and that can make the cells harder to kill with cytotoxic chemotherapy or radiation [4]. Moderate levels of intracellular oxidative stress often act to reinforce these changes, by causing temporary inhibition of phosphatases that remove tyrosine phosphate groups.

Cancer cells are distinguished by the fact that, owing to mutagenic alterations in their DNA, or so-called epigenetic (potentially reversible) changes in their DNA structure, the amount of certain proteins made by these cells is increased or decreased, and/or the structure of these proteins is altered in ways that influence their function [5]. In cancer, the net impact of these changes is to boost the activity of signal transduction mechanisms that support cellular multiplication, tissue invasion, and metastasis to distant organs, and that protect the cells from being killed by radiation or chemotherapy. Often, cancer cells express increased amounts of cell receptors, phosphorylate tyrosines, or make mutant receptors that are constantly active in this regard [6-8]. The pro-growth, pro-survival impacts of these receptors are often amplified by increased oxidant stress in cancer cells, which prevents phosphatase enzymes from turning off the signals triggered by these receptors [9,10].

One of the goals at Oasis of Hope is to use nutrients, phytochemicals, and currently available drugs to suppress signal transduction pathways that are overactive in cancer cells, or boost pathways that are underactive. The intent is for cancer cells to grow slower, make them aggressive, or make them easier to destroy.

7
. . .

Oxidative Pre-conditioning Therapy: Ozone and UV Light

When most people hear the word ozone, they think of a protective layer of the atmosphere but aren't really sure what it is beyond that. Ozone is oxygen but with the molecular structure O3 instead of O2. This additional molecule makes ozone a highly reactive oxidant. If inhaled, ozone can do some serious damage to our bodies. However, there is an application of this substance that is very therapeutic. But first, let's take a closer look at ozone.

In nature, ozone has a good side and a bad side. In the stratosphere, it acts as a shield, deflecting harmful UV irradiation. However, in the troposphere, ozone is a major component of the smog that harms humans, animals, and plants. When we breathe it, ozone can cause serious pulmonary and systemic side effects because it is such a powerful oxidant.

On the world scene, ozone therapy became an innovative medical approach in 1954, when Wehrly and Steinbart first described its application. They found that while the human respiratory tract reacts very negatively to ozone, human blood does not. In fact, when exposed to appropriate ozone concentrations, our blood tames the strong oxidant properties of ozone, thus eliminating any acute side effects. The benefits derived from this therapy are staggering.

The ozone autohemotherapy (O3-AHT) standard technique is to withdraw 150-200 ml of blood and expose it to an oxygen/ozone mixture at a specified ozone concentration, followed by intravenous reinfusion of this blood into the patient.

Ozone rapidly decomposes in blood to generate reactive oxygen compounds that act as an oxidative stimulus to the body and interact immediately with several substances, namely fatty acids, cholesterol, proteins, and carbohydrates.

An important role of O3-AHT in the Oasis of Hope IRT protocols is to serve as a technique for "oxidative preconditioning" [1]. Exposing cells to an acute and repeated mild oxidant stress typically leads to a compensatory increase in antioxidant defenses. This increase in tolerance to oxidative stress can be protective if a subsequent stronger oxidative stress is applied. Although the only cells exposed to oxidative stress during O3-AHT are the blood cells that are directly mixed with ozone [2] and reinfused, it seems likely that these cells will generate by-products of oxidant stress that other cells can "interpret" as signs of oxidative damage. This leads to induction of antioxidant defenses. In fact, several studies show that, when rats are pre-exposed to ozone (usually by rectal administration), they subsequently are protected from various oxidant stressors, including the chemotherapy drug cisplatin, the hepatotoxin carbon tetrachloride, the diabetes-inducing drug streptozotocin, endotoxin, and a brief cut-off of blood flow (ischemia-reperfusion) [3-8]. In the study with cisplatin, it was intriguing that the ozone pretreatment did not influence that antioxidant status of the kidney in healthy rats. But, in rats treated with cisplatin, it prevented a decrease in kidney antioxidants (glutathione and antioxidant enzymes) seen in the rats given cisplatin without O3-AHT pretreatment; O3-AHT also maintained normal kidney function in the cisplatin-treated rats [3].

In addition to cisplatin, a number of chemotherapy agents are known to generate oxidant stress in the body. This stress can contribute to the damage to healthy tissues that can make chemotherapy a traumatic experience and limit the doses that can be used. For this reason, Oasis of Hope employs O3-AHT as an "oxidative preconditioning" strategy in an effort to limit the damaging impact of chemotherapy to healthy tissues such as the bone marrow, intestinal tract, kidney, and heart.

In addition to treating blood with ozone, we also expose it to ultraviolet light before reinfusing it into the patient. This is intended to boost the generation of oxidative stress and thereby improve the efficacy of oxidative preconditioning therapy. Without question, ozone therapy is rapidly becoming an essential tool for oncologists and an integral part of comprehensive treatment programs.

8
∎ ∎ ∎
The IRT Anti-Inflammatory Therapies

The Oasis of Hope IRTs make use of three anti-inflammatory drugs, each of which has been in use for decades: salsalate, disulfiram, and diclofenac. These drugs are used to target key proteins that, in many cancers, promote cancer growth and spread while inducing resistance to chemotherapy or radiotherapy.

Pro-inflammatory Factors

One of these targets is known as "NF-kappaB." This protein complex regulates the synthesis of a number of other proteins by binding to DNA in the cellular nucleus. In a high proportion of advanced cancers, NF-kappaB is either continuously activated or is rapidly activated in response to chemotherapy [1-5]. One of the most important roles of NF-kappaB is to boost the production of a number of proteins that act in a variety of ways to prevent the process of apoptosis. This is the "cell suicide" process that is the most common way in which cytotoxic anti-cancer drugs kill cancer cells [6]. Moreover, NF-kappaB also increases production of a "multi-drug resistance" membrane protein that functions to "pump" various cytotoxic chemicals, including many anti-cancer drugs, out of cells [7]. For these reasons, NF-kappaB activation, either chronic, or triggered by chemotherapy, tends to protect cancer cells during chemotherapy. Conversely, many studies show that inhibitors of NF-kappaB activity can make resistant cancer cells much more sensitive to chemotherapy and/or radiation [8-11].

Chronic activation of NF-kappaB also makes cancers act more aggressively. This reflects: increased production of

"angiogenic factors" that promote the development of new blood vessels required for cancer growth; increased production of proteolytic enzymes which enable cancer cells to penetrate and migrate through tissues; and increased production of certain factors that promote rapid cellular multiplication [12].
The bottom line is that cancers, which have evolved high NF-kappaB activity, tend to spread more rapidly and aggressively, and they are harder to kill off.

Another cancer protein which Oasis of Hope IRT's target is cyclooxygenase-2, more conveniently referred to as "cox-2." Cox-2 is an enzyme that functions to generate a group of hormone-like compounds known as prostanoids, many of which have inflammatory and pain-promoting activity. That's why inhibitors of cox-2 are frequently used to treat inflammatory conditions. However, many cancers also express elevated activity of cox-2 [13]. Some of the prostanoids it produces have growth factor activity for these cancers [14]. This growth factor activity promotes increased cancer proliferation, boosts angiogenesis, and also can make cancers harder to kill [15-19]. Furthermore, some prostanoids have local immunosuppressive activity that blunts the effectiveness of immune cells that attack the tumor [20].

It should be noted that both NF-kappaB and cox-2 play a direct role in angiogenesis. Activation of these factors occurs in endothelial cells – the cells that give rise to new blood vessels – during the angiogenic process. Angiogenesis is required for efficient production of new blood vessels [21-23]. Thus, inhibition of these proteins has the potential to directly suppress angiogenesis by targeting endothelial cell function.

As if NF-kappaB weren't already pernicious enough for cancer patients, this factor is now known to be a key mediator of the muscle protein loss associated with cancer cachexia [24]. Thus, effective inhibition of NF-kappaB likely has the potential to help cancer patients preserve their muscle mass.

Salsalate

Fortunately, several drugs are available which can suppress the activity of either NF-kappaB or cox-2. One of these is salicylic acid, a natural compound found in white willow bark that has been used for many decades to treat inflammatory disorders such as rheumatoid arthritis. In the late nineteenth century, German chemists first synthesized aspirin (acetylsalicylic acid) by adding an acetyl group to salicylic acid. Salicylic acid, like aspirin, can inhibit cyclooxygenase enzymes, but its activity in this regard is very weak and reversible, for which reason salicylic acid doesn't produce the dangerous side effects sometimes seen with chronic use of aspirin or related drugs, such as bleeding stomach ulcers or kidney damage [25-27]. It is now known that the anti-inflammatory effects of high-dose salicylic acid are more likely to reflect inhibition of NF-kappaB activation. Salicylic acid binds to and inhibits an enzyme that is usually required for NF-kappaB activation [28,29].

Although pharmaceutical companies are working feverishly to develop expensive new inhibitors of NF-kappaB, few medical scientists have considered the possibility of using natural, inexpensive salicylate in cancer therapy [30]. There is, however, recent research establishing that salicylate has cancer-retardant and anti-angiogenic activity. At Oasis of Hope, we believe that salicylic acid has considerable potential for use in cancer therapy, to potentiate the efficacy of chemotherapy in certain cancers, to slow the growth and spread of cancer during at-home therapy, and to slow or prevent the progression of cachexic muscle degeneration [31,32].

Several pharmaceutical forms of salicylic acid are available. We have chosen to use salsalate, a complex which is broken down in the intestinal tract to release free salicylic acid, which is then absorbed [33].

Salsalate is less likely to induce gastric irritation that other forms of salicylic acid. It was developed in Japan about 50 years ago, and has been in use since that time for treatment of inflammatory disorders. Salsalate won't produce dangerous toxicity when used as directed. However, in optimally effective anti-inflammatory doses, it can produce reversible ear dysfunction – tinnitus and mild hearing loss [34]. Fortunately, these problems resolve as soon as the drug is discontinued, and no permanent damage is done. For the occasional patient in whom these side effects are highly troubling, a dosage reduction can often solve the problem. It is necessary to use these high doses to achieve effective inhibition of NF-kappaB.

Disulfiram

Another drug with potential for inhibiting NF-kappaB is disulfiram – the drug more commonly known as "Antabuse." This drug was developed many years ago to help alcoholics abstain from alcohol. If they drink alcohol while using Antabuse, they become ill, owing to increased blood levels of the alcohol metabolite acetaldehyde. More recently, it has been discovered that disulfiram can inhibit cellular components known as proteasomes [35,36]. Proteasomes are responsible for degrading cellular proteins which have been specifically targeted for degradation. They play a crucial role in the activation of NF-kappaB by degrading a protein that inhibits this activation. Thus, inhibition of proteasome function usually decreases NF-kappaB activity [37]. Recent studies show that disulfiram and related sulfur-containing compounds can inhibit proteasomes and thereby suppress NF-kappaB activity in cancer cells. This renders them less aggressive and more susceptible to eradication [36]. In usual clinical doses, disulfiram is a reasonably well tolerated drug as long as the patient does not drink any alcoholic beverage. The dose-limiting toxicity is gastrointestinal upset.

Diclofenac

With respect to cox-2, there are many drugs, commonly referred to as NSAIDs, which can inhibit this enzyme. Some of these drugs are relatively selective to cox-2 – including the prominently advertised drugs Vioxx and Celebrex. In other words, these drugs have little impact on the other form of cyclooxygenase (cox-1). Prolonged effective inhibition of cox-1 can lead to serious complications such as bleeding stomach ulcerations and kidney damage. For that reason, pharmaceutical companies developed cox-2-specific inhibitors for use in the treatment of inflammatory disorders.

Instead of using the expensive, highly advertised and relatively new cox-2-specific inhibitors Celebrex or Vioxx, we at Oasis of Hope have decided to use a much older drug, diclofenac. Diclofenac has an activity spectrum nearly identical to that of Celebrex, producing effective inhibition of cox-2 in concentrations that only modestly impact cox-1, but it is much less expensive [38]. When administered in standard clinical doses, diclofenac is more effective than Vioxx at inhibiting cox-2 in the human body [39]. While diclofenac has recently been shown to increase heart attack risk like other cox-2-specific inhibitors do [40], we always use it in conjunction with low-dose aspirin, which likely will largely offset that risk.

9
■ ■ ■

Metronomic Therapy

In 2000, two cancer research groups published a remarkable observation, in tumor-bearing rodents, low-dose chemotherapy, too low to evoke side effects or have a meaningful direct impact on tumor cells, when given on a daily or near-daily schedule, could markedly retard tumor growth [1,2]. This proved to be true even when the tumors were known to be resistant to the chemotherapeutic drugs employed. The solution to this riddle was that the chemotherapy was slowing or preventing angiogenesis.

During angiogenesis, new endothelial cells are extremely fragile as they branch off from existing blood vessels, multiply, migrate into a tumor in response to chemical signals secreted by tumor cells, and eventually form themselves into tubular structures to give rise to new vessels. Whereas the endothelial cells lining established vessels only rarely multiply, are stabilized by growth factors provided by neighboring cells, and are rarely killed by clinically feasible doses of chemotherapy drugs. The endothelial cells engaged in angiogenesis are extremely sensitive to killing by these drugs, much more so than most cancer cells. Thus, when low-dose chemotherapy is administered on a daily schedule (known as "metronomic" because it is regular and even like the beat of a metronome) the continual death of endothelial cells attempting to form new blood vessels can substantially disrupt the angiogenic process, slowing it down notably.

One of the particular merits of this metronomic approach centers around cancer drug resistance. Whereas conventional, high-dose chemotherapy tends to select tumor cells that are resistant to the drugs used, metronomic chemotherapy targets normal endothelial cells that do not grow resistant to the drugs.

In other words, metronomic chemotherapy keeps on working when conventional therapy fails. Tumors may be able to adapt to a degree by increasing their production of pro-angiogenic factors that promote endothelial cell's survival. This explains why cancers, which initially regress in response to metronomic therapy, sometimes grow back despite continuing therapy. The cancer confers this relative resistance; not the endothelial cells themselves.

Recently, a further benefit of metronomic chemotherapy has been established. It tends to selectively kill a population of immune cells, called "T-reg" cells, that function to suppress the activity of immune cells capable of attacking the tumor. These are the natural killer (NK) cells and T-cytotoxic cells [3]. T-reg cells often congregate within tumors and secrete hormone-like factors that "turn off" the immune cells trying to attack the cancer. Thus, metronomic chemotherapy has emerged as a useful adjuvant to therapeutic strategies intended to boost the tumor-killing capacity of NK and T-cytotoxic cells [4,5].

The utility of treating rodent tumors, including transplanted human tumors, with metronomic chemotherapy has now been confirmed in a great many studies [6,7]. In some of these studies, combining such chemotherapy with other measures attacking the angiogenic process has led to complete remissions of pre-existing aggressive tumors [2,8]. Other studies also showed that metronomic chemotherapy can be useful when used in conjunction with conventional chemotherapy [9].

The most extensive published clinical experience with metronomic chemotherapy regimens has been provided by oncologists in Milan, who have documented the long-term responses of patients with metastatic breast cancer to a metronomic regimen involving daily cyclophosphamide (50mg) and two weekly doses of methotrexate (5mg per dose) [10,11].

From the patients using this regimen, 32% achieved either a complete or partial remission, or a stabilization of disease lasting at least 24 weeks. In about 16% of patients, no tumor progression was noted for over a year. Even in the patients in whom progression did occur, it seems likely that the therapy was often slowing the spread of the disease. The especially good news, since metronomic chemotherapy is intended for long-term use, is that this regimen was essentially free of annoying side effects. Only a mild suppression of white cell count was observed in a small minority of the treated patients.

Since metronomic therapy is directed against endothelial cells, not cancer cells, a metronomic regimen that works well with one type of cancer should work well with all types of cancer dependent on angiogenesis for growth. At Oasis of Hope, we use a metronomic regimen like that tested by the Milanese doctors. It is based on cyclophosphamide, also known by its trade name "Genoxal." We also include methotrexate for selected patients.

The Oasis of Hope IRT at-home protocols include additional agents intended to slow the process of angiogenesis. These include salsalate, silymarin, fish oil, the glycine in GPG, and the green tea polyphenols in Synerpax. Thus, we are attacking angiogenesis from as many angles as we feasibly can.

10

▪ ▪ ▪

IRT Nutraceuticals for Cancer Control

At Oasis of Hope, we employ a broad spectrum of safe nutraceuticals. They are used as components of the in-hospital therapy and for continuing use when patients return home. These agents are intended to modulate cell signaling pathways in ways that should provide a diverse array of benefits such as sensitizing cancers to cytotoxic chemotherapies or intravenous vitamin C, slowing the growth of tumors, blocking the process of metastasis, inhibiting the angiogenic response required for tumor growth, boosting or disinhibiting the immune system's capacity to attack the cancer, protecting normal tissues from the toxicity of chemotherapies, and helping to control so-called "paraneoplastic" syndromes that erode bones or decrease muscle mass. Here are the chief nutraceuticals we use with the explanation of why and how they are used.

Melatonin

Melatonin is a natural hormone produced primarily by the pineal gland at the base of the brain. Secretion of melatonin is regulated by light exposure. Also, a burst of melatonin secretion occurs at nighttime during the onset of sleep. One of the primary roles of melatonin is to synchronize endocrine and nervous system rhythms in line with day-night cycles. For this reason, melatonin is traditionally given at bedtime so that natural biorhythms are reinforced rather than disrupted.
Melatonin exerts a range of physiological effects, some of which are of direct relevance to cancer therapy.

Of particular interest is its ability to boost the function of NK cells and helper-T lymphocytes. These components of the immune system can help to control the growth and spread of many tumors [1,2]. NK cells usually have little impact on large pre-existing tumors, but they do a better job of controlling the small nests of tumor cells that can give rise to new metastases [3,4]. NK cell activity tends to decline as people age. This is at least partially attributable to the fact that the pineal's production of melatonin tends to decline during the aging process [5].

Melatonin also functions as a major antioxidant. Although melatonin itself can function as a free radical scavenger, this effect is probably of little physiological significance because natural concentrations of melatonin are quite low. The major impact of melatonin on antioxidant defenses reflects its ability to boost the production of many antioxidant enzymes in many tissues [6,7]. This antioxidant effect of melatonin can provide protection when cancer patients receive cytotoxic drugs that can damage healthy tissues by inducing oxidant stress. In experimental studies, melatonin administration has been shown to lessen the adverse effects of drugs such as doxorubicin and cisplatin, without lessening the therapeutic impact of these drugs [8-11]. The heart, kidneys, and peripheral nervous system are among the vital organs that melatonin protects.

Melatonin also functions to support the growth and survival of bone marrow cells that give rise to circulating neutrophils, lymphocytes, monocytes, which are immune cells, and platelets, which are required for proper blood clotting. It apparently does this by boosting the marrow's production of certain key growth factors [12,13]. This effect is of evident relevance to cancer therapy since many cytotoxic cancer drugs are highly toxic to the bone marrow. The resulting decline in blood levels of white cells or of platelets can increase risk for infection or bleeding complications, and may require chemotherapy to be terminated or postponed. This would impair its therapeutic efficacy.

Melatonin has been tested in clinical trials in a wide range of cancers. Sometimes it is used as a stand-alone therapy in patients for whom further chemotherapy would be inappropriate, and sometimes as an adjuvant to standard chemotherapy or radiotherapy regimens. In general, the results of these studies have been remarkably consistent [14-18]. With or without concurrent chemotherapy, the patients receiving melatonin tended to survive significantly longer. When chemotherapy was administered, therapeutic response, defined as objective remission or stable disease, tended to be significantly greater in those getting the melatonin. Furthermore, side effects of chemotherapy tended to be less severe in the melatonin group. In particular they were less prone to severe bone marrow depression. Chemotherapy with melatonin was also less likely to damage the heart or peripheral nervous system. Also, the patients receiving melatonin were less prone to cachexia, the severe loss of muscle mass that often complicates advanced cancer [19].

Given the scope of these benefits, it is remarkable that nocturnally administered melatonin appears to be virtually free of side effects. Some people report that melatonin helps them to remember their dreams more vividly. Aside from this, it tends to be well tolerated, and some people find that it helps them to get a restful night's sleep. Moreover, in light of the age-related fall-off in melatonin secretion, supplemental melatonin may be particularly beneficial to the overall health of people who are middle-aged or older. It supports improved immune and antioxidant defenses.

Cancer patients at Oasis of Hope frequently report that their experiences with chemotherapy tend to be less harsh and traumatic than were their previous chemotherapy regimens at other hospitals. We suspect that our inclusion of melatonin in the IRT protocols has a lot to do with this.

Fish Oil

Fish oil is a uniquely rich source of the long-chain omega-3 fatty acids EPA (eicosapentaenoic acid) and DHA (docosahexaenoic acid). A small structural difference distinguishes these fatty acids from the omega-6 fatty acids found in plant-derived oils. Within our bodies, a portion of ingested omega-6 fatty acids are converted to the compound arachidonic acid. This in turn is the precursor for a wide range of hormone-like compounds, known as prostanoids, that play a key role in inflammatory processes. EPA and DHA are very similar in structure to arachidonic acid, and, when consumed in adequate amounts, they can act in various ways to antagonize the production of active prostanoids. For this reason, diets rich in fish oil tend to have anti-inflammatory effects in rheumatoid arthritis and certain other chronic inflammatory disorders[20]. Furthermore, one of the prostanoids whose production is antagonized by fish oil is thromboxane, which plays a role in blood clot formation by promoting aggregation of the platelets. This discovery led to speculation that the relatively low risk for heart attack among aboriginal Eskimos may reflect their high consumption of seafood rich in EPA and DHA [21]. Also, omega-3 fats reduce the risk to develop dangerous cardiac arrhythmias.

EPA and DHA have a valuable role to play in cancer treatment. A number of studies show that a diet rich in fish oil tends to slow tumor growth [22-25]. At least part of this effect can be attributed to a suppressive effect of fish oil on angiogenesis. Remember that angiogenesis is the process by which new blood vessels develop to enable the growth and spread of tumors [24-27]. EPA has been shown to decrease the expression of a key receptor required for response to the pro-angiogenic compound vascular endothelial growth factor (VEGF) [28].

Another key factor in angiogenesis is the enzyme Cox-2, which produces prostanoids required for vascular tube formation during the angiogenic process [29].

A high intake of fish oil has the potential to antagonize the role of Cox-2 in the angiogenic process by decreasing the production of Cox-2-derived prostanoids.

Fish oil also has the potential to act directly on tumor cells to slow their proliferation. In some tumors, prostanoids produced by Cox-2 or other enzymes known as lipoxygenases can promote the multiplication and spread of cancer cells and/or protect them from apoptosis [30,31]. Fish oil can antagonize the pro-proliferative activity of these prostanoids by suppressing their synthesis.

Fish oil has the ability to fend off cachexia, the severe loss of muscle mass that often complicates late-stage cancer [32-35]. Although cachexia usually entails a loss of appetite that can contribute to weight loss by decreasing calorie intake, the life-threatening selective loss of muscle mass often seen in cancer reflects a very specific inflammatory process in muscle fibers that is not seen in healthy dieters. It has been discovered that EPA interferes with the inflammatory mechanisms that cause loss of muscle mass.

Finally, a number of experimental studies demonstrate that fish oil, particularly DHA, can boost the responsiveness of cancer cells to chemotherapy and radiotherapy [36,37]. The mechanism of this effect is not well understood, but it is suspected that DHA, which is polyunsaturated and highly susceptible to oxidative damage, serves to amplify oxidative stress in cancer cells assaulted by cytotoxic chemicals or radiation. Cell culture studies suggest that normal healthy cells are less susceptible to this sensitizing effect of DHA for reasons that remain unclear. The potential impact of DHA on response to chemotherapy is one reason why fish oil is included in the in-hospital supplementation regimen for cancer patients at Oasis of Hope. Most of us have a lot of fat in our bodies, including the omega-6 fats for which EPA and DHA serve as functional antagonists.

For that reason, it usually takes at least several months for fish oil intake to achieve its maximal physiological effects. The ratio of omega-3 to omega-6 in the body's tissues is a key determinant of the efficacy of fish oil supplementation. A given daily dose of fish oil will presumably have a greater and faster impact in people who are maintaining their total daily fat intake low.

In summary, the ample EPA/DHA intake provided with the Oasis of Hope IRT protocols is intended to: suppress the angiogenic process required for the growth and spread of tumors; act directly on some susceptible cancers to slow their proliferation; help prevent loss of muscle mass (cachexia); and improve the responsiveness of cancers to certain chemotherapeutic agents or radiation.

Vitamin D

Growing evidence confirms that good vitamin D status not only decreases risk for many prominent cancers, but also can improve the results of chemotherapy and lengthen survival in people who already have cancer. Vitamin D is often called "the sunshine vitamin" because the skin manufactures it when rays of ultra violet (UV) light interact with a cholesterol precursor in the skin. The resulting compound is then quickly transformed in the liver to a derivative, calcidiol, which circulates in the blood. Calcidiol can also be produced from vitamin D obtained from supplements or foods. Calcidiol, per se, has little physiological activity. In order to do its metabolic job, calcidiol must be further transformed to calcitriol, which can bind to vitamin D receptors in the nucleus of cells. Most of the calcitriol found in the blood is produced in the kidneys.

Just within the last few years, scientists have learned that many types of epithelial cells (type of cells that give rise to most of the dangerous solid tumors) are capable of converting calcidiol to calcitriol and the rate of this conversion is proportional to blood calcidiol levels [38,39]. In other words, epithelial cells can make more calcitriol when vitamin D status is improved by effective sun exposure or with supplemental vitamin D. Increased calcitriol levels in epithelial cells reduce the risk that these cells will give rise to malignant tumors. This reflects the fact that calcitriol works in various ways to slow down the cell multiplication while also increasing the propensity of mutated cells to "commit suicide" [40].

People's vitamin D status tends to vary a great deal, primarily owing to the fact that the skin's capacity to manufacture vitamin D is influenced by a number of factors [41]. The UV content of sunlight declines during the winter and in northern latitudes the winter sunlight is virtually devoid of UV. Certain types of air pollution that absorb UV also decrease the UV content of sunlight. Furthermore, skin production of vitamin D is lower in people who fail to get much sun exposure, who are darkly complected, or who use artificial sunscreens to prevent UV-mediated skin damage. Most natural foods are essentially devoid of vitamin D unless it is included as an additive. Traditional supplemental doses of vitamin D, typically 400 IU daily, are so low that they are just sufficient to prevent rickets. Neither food nor supplementation has had much impact on vitamin D status in most people. Consider the fact that, with optimal UV exposure, people can make up to 10,000 -20,000 IU of vitamin D daily [42].

Since UV exposure is the chief determinant of vitamin D status for most people, it should follow that, if vitamin D activity has a major impact on cancer risk, logic would dictate that there would be a greater incidence for many cancers in parts of the world where UV exposure is often low. This, in fact, is precisely what epidemiologists have been demonstrating over the last decade [43-48].

In other words, people who have spent most of their lives in sunny regions, tend to be at lower risk for cancer than people who live in northern latitudes. It has been estimated that sub optimal UV exposure is responsible for over 23,000 premature cancer deaths per year in the U.S. alone [38,49]. The types of cancer whose risks are influenced by vitamin D status include cancers of the breast, colon, rectum, ovary, prostate, pancreas, stomach, and uterine endometrium, as well as non-Hodgkin's lymphoma.

But what does this have to do with therapy of pre-existing cancers? Fortunately, some of the cancers that arise from epithelial cells capable of making calcitriol retain the capacity to make calcitriol and express vitamin D receptors [38,50]. In these cancers, an increase in blood levels of calcidiol, achieved by better UV exposure or supplemental vitamin D, leads to an increased production of calcitriol in the tumor. This calcitriol can slow the proliferation of the cancer cells while increasing their ability to commit suicide [51-53]. Moreover, the impact of calcitriol on capacity for apoptosis can sometimes render these cancers more susceptible to cytotoxic chemotherapy or radiotherapy [54-57].

Recently, epidemiologists around the world have noted that cancer patients diagnosed during summer typically survive longer than patients diagnosed in winter [58-60]. This presumably reflects the fact that, in those cancers still capable of making calcitriol, the relatively good vitamin D status during summers renders the cancers more sensitive to chemotherapy and/or slows the growth of the cancer. At Oasis of Hope, we make sure that our patients are being treated "in summer" by giving them 10,000 IU of vitamin D daily.

One pioneering study from Toronto has examined the influence of supplemental vitamin D (2,000 IU daily) on prostate cancer patients whose PSA levels remained measurable following surgery or radiotherapy [61]. During this supplementation, the rate of tumor growth, assessed by PSA measurements, slowed markedly in 14 of the 15 subjects enrolled in the study.

Silibinin

Milk thistle extract has been used for many decades in the treatment of liver disorders. Approximately 80% of this extract consists of silymarin, a mixture of several compounds known as flavonolignans. Silibinin, the most prominent of these compounds, accounts for about 60% of the weight of silymarin, and is believed responsible for most of the liver-protective activity of silymarin and milk thistle extract. Just within the last decade, scientists have learned that silibinin has considerable potential for preventing and treating cancer.

In concentrations that may be feasible to achieve with high-dose clinical regimens, silibinin has been shown to have growth inhibitory effects on a wide range of human cancer cell lines including cancers arising from the prostate, breast, colon, lung, liver, bladder, and cervix [62-69]. Silibinin can suppress the proliferation of these cells, while at the same time increasing the rate at which they die by apoptosis. In addition, silibinin can sensitize cancer cell lines to the killing effects of certain cytotoxic chemotherapeutic drugs [70]. Thus, silibinin may have potential both for retarding the growth and spread of cancer and for boosting the response of cancers to chemotherapy.

The mechanisms responsible for these effects have been studied most intensively in human prostate cancer cells [71]. It should first be noted that these studies show that concentrations of silibinin, which retard the growth of these prostate cancers, do not influence the growth of cells from a normal healthy prostate. In other words, the effects of silibinin on cell proliferation appear to be specific to cancer cells. The anti-proliferative effects of silibinin on prostate cancer cells have been traced to a decreased function of the epidermal growth factor receptor (EGF-R).

This is a key mediator of growth signals in prostate cancer and in many other types of cancer [72]. Silibinin binds to this receptor and prevents it from interacting with hormones that activate it. Some of these are produced in prostate cancers. Furthermore, silibinin induces prostate cancer cells to make more of a compound, known as IGFBP-3, that binds to and inhibits the activity of insulin-like growth factor-I (IGF-I), a key growth factor for many cancers [73].

Silibinin has also been shown to decrease the activation of NF-kappaB [74,75], a protein complex that, when activated, tends to make cancer cells more aggressive and renders them less sensitive to chemotherapy or radiotherapy [76,77]. In many prostate cancers, and indeed in many other types of cancer, NF-kappaB is continuously active. The effect of silibinin on NF-kappaB helps to rationalize silibinin's ability to increase the sensitivity of cancers to certain chemotherapy drugs. The effects of silibinin on growth factor signals, which promote cancer cell survival, also contribute in this regard.

The impact of orally administered silibinin on the growth of human tumors in immunodeficient mice has been studied with three different types of tumor – prostate, lung, and ovarian [78,79]. In each case, silibinin has been found to have a substantial and dose-dependent suppressive effect on tumor growth in doses that had no apparent toxicity to the treated animals.

Examination of the silibinin-treated tumors revealed that they had a much less developed vasculature than control tumors. In other words, there were less blood vessels in the tumor to provide nourishment and oxygen [78,79].

Follow-up studies showed that in some cancers silibin could suppress secretion of a compound known as vascular endothelial growth factor (VEGF), which plays a key role in inducing the growth of new blood vessels into tumors [78,80,81].

Furthermore, other studies show that clinically feasible concentrations of silibinin have a direct effect on endothelial cells. Silibinin can suppress the proliferation of these cells and reduce their ability to migrate, invade tissues, and roll themselves into tubes, which is how new blood vessels are formed [74,80]. These findings suggest that the growth-slowing impact of silibinin on tumors reflects the interaction of at least three phenomena: a direct anti-proliferative effect on cancer cells; a suppression of VEGF production by these cells; and a direct inhibitory effect on the capacity of endothelial cells to build new blood vessels.

Selenium

The use of selenium in cancer therapy is motivated, in part, by substantial evidence that good selenium nutrition can reduce cancer risk [82]. Dr. Larry Clark, and colleagues, conducted a massive double blind clinical study that recruited over 1,300 American subjects known to be at high risk for skin cancer, but free of any serious cancers at the time of enrollment [83]. For over a decade, these volunteers received either selenium (200 mcg daily) or a matching placebo. Although the supplemental selenium failed to reduce subsequent risk for skin cancer, the researchers were encouraged to find that the cancer death rate in the selenium-supplemented group was only half as high as that in those receiving the placebo, 29 vs. 57. Indeed, the researchers were forced to terminate the study earlier than planned, as they considered it unethical to continue with the placebo supplementation. The lower cancer death rate in the selenium group was primarily attributable to a substantial reduction in the incidence of new serious cancers in the lungs, colon, and prostate[84,85].

Epidemiological studies have also pointed to decreased risks for certain cancers in people who have relatively high selenium intakes, or who live in regions of the world where soil selenium levels are relatively high [84,85].

One reason why people with poor selenium nutrition may be at increased cancer risk is that selenium is an important antioxidant nutrient that supports the production of enzymes that protect our cells against oxidant stress [86]. Since oxidants can damage DNA, leading to potentially carcinogenic mutations, good selenium status clearly has anti-mutagenic potential.

Of course, preventing cancer and treating cancer are two different things. In animal studies, selenium isn't as effective for controlling pre-existing cancers as it is for preventing cancer. But, the ability of selenium to prevent cancer in carcinogen-treated animals suggests that selenium administered in conjunction with chemotherapy may well reduce the chance that treatment with DNA-damaging cytotoxic agents could ultimately give rise to new cancers.

Furthermore, although selenium alone usually isn't effective as a cancer therapy, there is exciting recent evidence that, as an adjuvant to high doses of intravenous vitamin C, chemotherapy or radiotherapy, supplemental selenium can render cancer cells more sensitive to these measures, while simultaneously protecting normal healthy tissues [87,88]. By using selenium in conjunction with chemotherapy, scientists achieve higher cure rates in rodents with transplanted tumors. This is because the tumors become more sensitive to the chemotherapies, and because the researchers can use higher doses of the drugs without producing life-threatening toxicities. Clinical studies are now in progress at Roswell Park Memorial Hospital evaluating supplemental selenium as an adjuvant to chemotherapy regimens. Preliminary reports indicate that the selenium is helping to maintain effective white cell counts, reduce the need for transfusions, and decrease side effects such as nausea, vomiting, and hair loss [89]. The Roswell researchers are giving their chemotherapy patients 2,000mcg selenium daily prior to and during chemotherapy.

One recent study demonstrates that selenium protects normal cells from cytotoxin-mediated DNA damage by boosting the ability of a protective protein known as p53 to trigger DNA repair mechanisms in cells [89]. Since the p53 protein is absent in most advanced cancers, this might explain why the protective benefit of selenium is confined largely to normal cells.

A further reason for using selenium in cancer therapy is that high intakes of this mineral have been shown to boost immune responses. In particular, the types of immune cells involved in cancer control, cytotoxic T lymphocytes and NK cells, function more effectively with increased intakes of selenium [90,91].

In summary, the likely benefits of selenium in clinical cancer therapy, especially when used as an adjuvant to chemotherapy, are: improved response of cancers to chemotherapy and high doses of intravenous vitamin C; a reduction in chemotherapy side effects; increased capacity of the immune system to fight cancer spread; and reduced risk that chemotherapy may eventually give rise to a new cancer.

Synerpax

Synerpax is a multi-ingredient nutritional supplement used in conjunction with both the in-hospital and at-home IRT regimens. It provides a blend of phytochemicals: green tea polyphenols, curcumin, piperine, resveratrol, and grape seed extract. These have demonstrated cancer retardant efficacy. Synerpax also includes Selenium and Zinc, which are important elements in the fight against cancer.

Green Tea Extract

Perhaps the most clinically significant of these ingredients is green tea extract. The extract employed is highly potent, comprising 98% polyphenols, the most prominent of which is the compound epigallocatechin-gallate, better and more conveniently known as "EGCG." Recent research shows that EGCG can achieve worthwhile inhibition of an important receptor on endothelial cells in concentrations that can feasibly be reached after oral administration. The receptor in question responds to a crucial stimulant of angiogenesis, vascular endothelial growth factor (VEGF). Many cancer cells produce VEGF. It is such a key mediator of angiogenesis that several new hyper expensive cancer drugs target the bioactivity of VEGF. The strategy employed by Oasis of Hope is to attack angiogenesis from as many angles as feasible, in the hope that the cumulative effect will be a clinically worthwhile retardation of tumor growth [92-96].

Curcumin

Another intriguing phytochemical supplied by Synerpax is curcumin – the agent that makes turmeric yellow. Curcumin has slowed growth, promoted cell death by apoptosis, and increased responsiveness to chemotherapy drugs in a wide range of cancer cell lines [97-101]. Oral curcumin may indeed prove to have value for prevention of colon cancer [102], which reflects the fact that curcumin taken up by the mucosal cells lining the colon can exert a worthwhile effect in these cells before it is metabolized.

Piperine

To expedite the absorption of curcumin and perhaps other constituents of this supplement, Synerpax includes piperine, also known as Bioperine®. It is a compound found in black pepper. Piperine has been shown to enhance the absorption of numerous phytochemicals and drugs, in part because it is a potent inhibitor of a protein "pump" that pushes a wide range of chemicals out of intestinal cells [103]. A clinical study assessing absorption of curcumin found that concurrent administration of piperine improved absorption about 20-fold [104]. A favorable effect on piperine on absorption of EGCG in mice has also been reported[105].

Grape Seed Extract

Synerpax also provides grape seed extract and resveratrol. These agents, like EGCG and curcumin, have exerted favorable effects on cancer cells in culture. Grape seed extract is rich in antioxidant flavonoids known as proanthocyanidins. Recent studies show that a high oral intake of grape seed extract can markedly inhibit the growth of human colorectal and prostate cancers implanted in mice [106,107]. These findings suggest that, at some sufficiently high intake, grape seed extract may prove useful in clinical cancer therapy.

Resveratrol

Resveratrol is an antioxidant phytochemical found in red wine. Resveratrol, like curcumin, has potential to block the activation of NF-kappaB, a protein complex that makes many cancers more aggressive and resistant to chemotherapy [108].

Zinc

A nutritional dose of zinc is included in Synerpax since this mineral plays a key role in effective function of the immune system. It is desirable to insure that the zinc nutrition of cancer patients is at least adequate [109].

Boswellic Acids

Boswellic acids are a group of closely related compounds found in salai guggul, a resinous extract from the tree Boswellia carteri traditionally used in Ayurvedic (Indian) medicine as an anti-inflammatory agent [110]. In the early 1990s, German researchers discovered the mechanistic basis for salai guggul's anti-inflammatory efficacy. Boswellic acids are very potent inhibitors of the enzyme 5-lipoxygenase (5LPO), which plays an essential role in the generation of a family of hormone-like pro-inflammatory compounds known as leukotrienes [111].

There is increasing evidence that 5LPO is often expressed by many types of cancer, and that this enzyme generates compounds that have potent growth factor activities for these cancers [112-114]. Inhibiting 5LPO typically retards the growth of cancer cell lines dependent on 5LPO, and often increases the rate at which these cells die by apoptosis. Human cancer cell lines derived from prostatic, pancreatic, breast, esophageal, colorectal, bladder, gastric, and renal cancers, as well as mesotheliomas and leukemias, have shown 5LPO dependency [115-122]. Not all such cancers are 5LPO dependent.

The impact of 5LPO activity on the sensitivity of cancers to chemotherapy or radiotherapy has so far received little attention. However, one fascinating recent report indicates that, concurrent expression of 5LPO is associated with substantial protection from the cytotoxicity of chemotherapeutic cancer drugs [123].

Conversely, suppression of 5LPO in these cancers greatly enhances their sensitivity to these drugs. This implies that 5LPO inhibitors, administered prior to and during chemotherapy, should enhance the responsiveness of a high proportion of human cancers.

Zileuton, a drug approved for treatment of asthma, works by inhibiting 5LPO, and has shown cancer-retardant activity in hamsters with pancreatic cancer [124]. However, we have chosen to use boswellic acid-rich extracts in Oasis of Hope IRT regimens because they are considerably less expensive and can be presumed to be safe based on centuries of use in traditional medicine. Moreover, a number of cell culture studies indicate that boswellic acids, most notably one known as acetyl-11-keto-beta-boswellic acid, can slow the proliferation and boost the death rate of various human cancer cell lines [125-129]. The only published clinical experience with boswellic acids in the treatment of cancer dealt with the use of these agents in patients with progressing brain cancers [130,131]. Although some of the children experienced improved neurological function during this treatment, this might have reflected an anti-inflammatory effect of leukotriene suppression rather than tumor regression. Nonetheless, the observed benefit was worthwhile. In rats transplanted with gliomas, treatment with boswellic acids could more than double survival time [132]. In the in-hospital IRT protocol and at-home regimen, we include a potent dose of boswellic acids.

GPG

GPG is a nutraceutical, developed by Oasis of Hope scientists, that features Glycine, Modified Citrus Pectin and Glutamine. Recent research has demonstrated that these three active ingredients have the potential to: slow the growth and spread of cancer by blocking the processes of metastasis and angiogenesis, enhance the immune system, help prevent cachectic loss of muscle mass, and protect healthy tissues from the toxic effects of chemotherapy.

Glycine

Glycine is a non-essential amino acid that has a pleasant sweet flavor. Glycine doesn't target a tumor directly, but rather inhibits the process of angiogenesis [133-135].

Modified Citrus Pectin

Another key component of GPG is Modified Citrus Pectin (MCP). Pectin is a soluble fiber found in citrus fruits. MCP is a special form of pectin that has been partially hydrolyzed so that it is less branched and more absorbable.

Studies have shown that orally administered MCP can impede the metastatic spread of implanted tumors [136]. In order for metastasis to occur, cancer cells in the bloodstream must first attach themselves to the walls of small blood vessels. This binding is achieved by membrane proteins known as galectins [137,138]. Modified Citrus Pectin binds to galectins, blocking their ability to promote adherence of cancer cells to vessel's walls [139].

Galectins also play a role in the angiogenesis process by helping endothelial cells to roll up into tubes so that they can form new vessels [140]. In a recent clinical trial in patients with prostate cancer, the rate of tumor growth slowed significantly when the patients received MCP [141]. In studies with rodents, MCP showed the ability to block formation of new metastases.

Glutamine

The last ingredient of GPG is the amino acid glutamine. This amino acid serves as an important source of food calories for immune cells as well as the gastrointestinal tract. Skeletal muscle constantly generates and exports glutamine to aid the nutrition of these tissues [142].

Glutamine also has the potential to protect immune and gastrointestinal cells from damage by radiation and/or chemotherapy [143-145]. A recent study observed that supplemental glutamine helps the white blood cell count (neutrophils) to recover faster following chemotherapy [146].

The potential benefits of supplemental glutamine to cancer patients are multi-faceted: reducing some of the dangerous side effects of radiation and/or chemotherapy, without protecting tumor cells [143-147]; boosting the capacity of natural killer cells to attack the tumor, thereby helping to control the spread of cancer, particularly new metastases; and helping to prevent the severe loss of muscle mass (cachexia), a common complication of advanced cancer.

Biotin

Most tumors have a rather haphazard blood supply that leaves some regions of the tumor poorly perfused and low in oxygen. It has long been known that when cancer cells are in a hypoxic environment, they tend to be less sensitive, not only to radiotherapy, but also chemotherapy. The basis of this phenomenon has not been fully clarified, but scientists recently have proposed an intriguing explanation [148-151]. Most tumors generate a gaseous compound known as nitric oxide, which has a range of important physiological effects. Synthesis of nitric oxide can be substantially reduced in hypoxic tumor regions since oxygen is required for the production of this compound [152,153]. Researchers have reported that adding small amounts of nitric oxide (or rather chemicals like glyceryl trinitrate, which generate this volatile compound) to cancer cells incubated in low oxygen, can substantially boost the ability of cytotoxic chemotherapy drugs to kill these cells. Conversely, in cancer cells that are normally oxygenated, administration of drugs which inhibit production of nitric oxide reduces the sensitivity of these cells to cytotoxic chemicals – in effect, mimicking the impact of low oxygen exposure. Thus, it is now believed that the reduction in tumor production of nitric oxide associated with tumor hypoxia is largely responsible for the diminished sensitivity of cancer cells to chemotherapy in hypoxic tumor regions.

Importantly, adding a source of extra nitric oxide to cells that are normally oxygenated does not seem to alter their sensitivity to cytotoxic chemotherapy [148]. Evidently, whereas a small amount of nitric oxide is needed for optimal chemosensitivity, excess amounts do not further boost this sensitivity. Thus, clinical strategies which increase levels of nitric oxide throughout the body or which mimic the physiological effects of this compound, would not be expected to increase the toxic impact of chemotherapy on normally oxygenated healthy tissues.

One of the chief physiological effects of nitric oxide is to activate the enzyme guanylate cyclase, which generates an important regulatory compound known as cyclic GMP. This appears to be the main mediator of nitric oxide's favorable impact on cancer chemosensitivity [148]. Thus, measures which boost cyclic GMP production in hypoxic cancer cells increase their chemosensitivity the way that nitric oxide does.

How should this new knowledge be applied in cancer therapy? One recent study shows that the ability of doxorubicin, a cytotoxic chemotherapy drug, to control the growth of a transplanted human prostate cancer in mice, is significantly enhanced if the mice are concurrently treated with glyceryl trinitrate patches that boost levels of nitric oxide throughout the body [151].

Although it would probably be feasible for us to use similar patches in conjunction with chemotherapy, we have chosen a somewhat more elegant, more natural, and less expensive approach – high-dose biotin. Biotin is a physiologically essential B vitamin. However, in concentrations roughly ten-fold higher than physiological levels, biotin acts as a direct activator of guanylate cyclase [154]. In other words, biotin mimics the impact of nitric oxide in this regard, boosting production of cyclic GMP. In light of the fact that biotin appears to be quite safe, even in high doses, we have decided to use mega-dose biotin as a nitric oxide mimetic, in an effort to boost the chemotherapeutic responsiveness of poorly-oxygenated cancer cells.

11
■ ■ ■
IRT Nutraceuticals for Specific Cancers

Not all cancers are alike. Each type of cancer has its own special properties. That's why some phytonutrients have the potential to aid control of certain cancers, but not others. Thus, the Oasis of Hope IRT regimens include some agents that are used only for the treatment of one or several specific cancers. Agents that fall into this category include soy isoflavones, lycopene, pomegranate extract, coenzyme Q10, resveratrol, curcumin, and biotin.

Soy Isoflavones

There are two types of estrogen receptors: alpha and beta [1]. The alpha form of the receptor (ERalpha) tends to have growth promotional activity in tissues that express it. Thus, when estrogens activate ERalpha in breast or the uterus (endometrium), they promote proliferation and increase the risk that a cancer will arise in the stimulated tissue. Once a cancer does arise, estrogens tend to support the growth and survival of the cancer cells – at least until the tumor evolves to "estrogen independence." By way of contrast, the beta form of the estrogen receptor (ERbeta) tends to have anti-proliferative actions. In the tissues, which express it, activation of ERbeta helps to prevent cancer, and, in cancers which express ERbeta, its activation tends to slow cancer spread and improve therapeutic response [2]. There is, however, a tendency for expression of ERbeta to decline as cancers evolve over time. This adaptation likely reflects selection for more aggressive cancer cells [3-5].

Epithelial cells of the colon, prostate, and ovary tissues that express ERbeta are not usually thought of as estrogen responsive. The cancers that arise from these tissues often continue to express ERbeta, and can be controlled to some degree by estrogens which activate ERbeta [6-12]. While it is well known that postmenopausal estrogen replacement therapy increases the risk for breast cancer, it is less appreciated that such therapy reduces risk for colorectal cancer. This presumably reflects the protective activity of ERbeta [13].

Using estrogenic drugs to control colorectal, prostate, or ovarian cancers is a less than ideal proposition. Such hormones would have feminizing effects in men and could increase risk for breast or uterine cancer in women. Thus, it is extremely fortunate that soy isoflavones preferentially activate ERbeta, in serum concentrations that can feasibly be achieved by heavy ingestion of soy products or the use of concentrated supplements, but that have very little impact on ERalpha [1,2]. That's why soy-rich diets don't feminize men, but still have "phytoestrogen" activity.

These considerations help to rationalize the numerous epidemiological studies which conclude that people whose diets are relatively rich in soy products are at lower risk for colorectal, prostate, or ovarian cancer [14-16]. They also help to explain why diets high in soy or soy isoflavones tend to reduce the incidence of these cancers in carcinogen-treated rodents [17-19]. Such diets also can inhibit the growth of transplanted human prostate tumors, and/ or render these cancers more sensitive to control by chemo- or radiotherapy [20].

More importantly, several pilot clinical trials in men with prostate cancer and steadily rising PSA values have shown that soy isoflavones or a soy-rich diet can slow the rise in PSA in some instances causing a moderate temporary reduction in this biomarker [21].

Lycopene

The role for dietary lycopene in the prevention and treatment of prostate cancer was first suggested by epidemiological studies pointing to a decrease in risk for serious prostate cancer in men who consumed an ample amount of tomato products [22]. Tomatoes are very rich in the carotenoid lycopene, and tomato products represent the chief source of lycopene in most diets. Subsequent studies showed that diets enriched in lycopene could slow the growth of transplanted human prostate cancers in mice [23]. Moreover, two clinical reports from India indicate that surprisingly modest daily doses of lycopene can reduce or slow the rise in PSA in patients with metastatic prostate cancer [24,25]. In a Dutch controlled clinical study targeting patients with rising PSA despite recent prostatectomy, a complex dietary supplement featuring lycopene, soy isoflavones, silymarin, and antioxidants was shown to slow the rate of PSA increase [26]. All of these nutraceuticals are included in Oasis of Hope IRT regimens for prostate cancer. Another study showed that heavy consumption of tomato products by patients scheduled for prostatectomy can exert an antioxidant effect on the prostate, reducing the level of oxidatively damaged DNA [27]. This suggests that lycopene, and perhaps other constituents in tomato sauce, may play a physiologically important role in protecting the prostate from oxidative damage.

Pomegranate Extract

The other tumor-specific nutraceutical that Oasis of Hope uses with prostate cancer patients is pomegranate extract. Although most pomegranate research has focused on potential benefits for cardiovascular health, the possibility that pomegranate extracts could influence the induction and growth of cancer is now receiving attention. Indeed, two recent studies have demonstrated that oral administration of pomegranate fruit extract can slow the growth of transplanted human prostate cancers [28,29]. These favorable findings are now complemented by a recent clinical study in which patients with rising PSA values after initial treatment were asked to drink 8 ounces of pomegranate juice daily. Subsequently, a marked slowing of tumor growth was observed [30]. In light of these promising recent findings, the Oasis of Hope IRT protocols for prostate cancer patients now include pomegranate fruit extract daily.

Pomegranate extract may ultimately prove to have broader utility in cancer management. For example, there are recent reports that oral administration of pomegranate fruit extract slows the growth of a transplanted human lung cancer, as well as of lung cancers induced in mice by carcinogen pre-treatment [31,32]. If further positive reports are forthcoming, we may broaden the use of pomegranate extract in Oasis of Hope IRT protocols.

Coenzyme Q10

During the 1970s, the antioxidant nutrient coenzyme Q10 (CoQ) began to attract attention as a possible adjuvant for cancer therapy. This interest was prompted initially by several studies showing that CoQ supplementation could boost the function of macrophages, immune cells that help to recruit other types of immune cells that can attack cancers [33,34]. Subsequently, physicians affiliated with CoQ expert Dr. Karl Folkers began to employ CoQ, in doses as high as 390 mg daily, in the treatment of patients with metastatic breast cancer. Several of these patients were reported to experience complete or partial regression of metastases while on CoQ therapy [35,36]. In addition, a study found that 38% of patients with metastatic breast cancer had serum levels of CoQ that were abnormally low [37].

Resveratrol

Another nutraceutical potentially useful in breast cancer is resveratrol. This phytonutrient, a key antioxidant in wine, is included in Synerpax, and is discussed elsewhere in that context. So far, the only type of transplanted human cancer that has been shown to respond to resveratrol is breast cancer [38].

Curcumin

Another key ingredient of Synerpax is curcumin. This phytonutrient seems likely to have its greatest impact on colorectal or intestinal cancers that are still in their original location, not having been removed surgically. Under these circumstances, curcumin may be able to reach some of the cancer cells before it has been extensively metabolized in the process of absorption.

Biotin

Oasis of Hope at-home supplementation for colorectal cancer includes high doses of the B vitamin biotin. This is because moderately high concentrations of this vitamin can activate the enzyme guanylate cyclase, which produces an intracellular regulatory compound called cyclic GMP (cGMP). Many studies show that cGMP slows the rate of proliferation of colon cancer cells, while increasing their tendency to "commit suicide" via apoptosis. Increased production of cGMP also appears likely to reduce risk for colorectal cancer. Why these beneficial effects of cGMP appear to be specific for colorectal cancer remains unclear.

12
...
IRT Specific Drugs for Cancer Control

Oasis of Hope IRT protocols, in addition to including a range of anti-inflammatory adjuvant drugs, also include several other drugs that usually are not considered anti-inflammatory. These include the drugs cimetidine and valproic acid, each of which has been used safely for decades. We also use drugs that modulate sex hormone activities in patients who have hormone-sensitive breast or prostate cancers. The following provides an explanation.

Cimetidine

Cimetidine, also known as Tagamet, has been in wide use for many years as a treatment for gastrointestinal ulcers. It functions to suppress production of gastric acid by blocking so-called H2 receptors for the hormone histamine. In 1988, Danish researchers reported that, in patients with gastric cancer, concurrent cimetidine therapy was associated with improved survival [1]. Since then, cimetidine has been reported to improve survival in patients with colorectal cancer [2,3] and occasional objective responses have been observed in patients with melanoma or renal cell cancer treated with cimetidine alone or in conjunction with the anti-coagulant drug coumari. [4,5]. Cimetidine has also shown growth-retardant effects on certain cancers in rodents [6,7]. It was initially suspected that these benefits reflected a significant role for histamine as an immunosuppressive or growth-stimulant hormone in clinical cancer. However, cancer clinical studies evaluating other anti-ulcer drugs that block H2 receptors failed to show survival benefits, suggesting that the favorable responses to cimetidine might reflect an idiosyncratic effect of this drug unrelated to histamine antagonism [8,9].

Since the incidence of metastases was found to be substantially decreased in colorectal cancer patients treated with cimetidine, Japanese researchers suspected that cimetidine might influence the capacity of cancer cells to bind to endothelial cells, an essential step in the formation of new metastases. They were in fact able to demonstrate that clinical concentrations of cimetidine did inhibit the adhesion of certain cancer cells to endothelial cells. This reflected cimetidine's ability to suppress endothelial expression of a key adhesion protein known as E-selectin [10]. E-selectin is able to bind to certain types of complex carbohydrate chains that are frequently expressed on the surfaces of cancer cells that have the capacity to metastasize, but not by the healthy tissues from which they arise [11]. In fact, the Japanese researchers were able to demonstrate that cimetidine treatment only improved the survival of colorectal cancer patients whose tumors expressed these types of carbohydrate chains [3]. Moreover, they showed that pre-treatment with cimetidine suppressed the formation of liver metastases in mice injected with cancer cells [10]. So it seems that cimetidine makes endothelial cells more "slippery" by suppressing the E-selectin adhesion protein, thus making it harder for cancer cells circulating in the bloodstream to bind to the endothelial lining of blood vessels. Other H2-antagonist anti-ulcer drugs did not influence E-selectin expression by endothelial cells – consistent with the failure of these drugs to influence survival in clinical cancer [10].

One fascinating clinical study concluded that administration of cimetidine for only a one-week period, prior to and following surgery, improved the prognosis of colorectal cancer patients [12]. This likely reflects the fact that the inflammatory response triggered by surgery induces increased expression of E-selectin by endothelial cells, while surgery also can dislodge cancer cells, increasing the number of such cells circulating in the blood. [11]. So the days immediately following surgery may be associated with high risk for new metastasis formation. Cimetidine administration at this time may thus be particularly protective.

This "slippery endothelium" hypothesis helps to explain how cimetidine works to prevent metastases and prolong survival in many types of cancer. However, it doesn't completely explain cimetidine's impact on cancer, because in some animal studies cimetidine has slowed the growth of the primary tumor. This appears to reflect an inhibitory impact of cimetidine on the angiogenic process that is essential for the growth of solid tumors. Thus, one recent study shows that, in mice bearing transplanted colon cancers, cimetidine therapy decreases the vascularity of the tumor [13]. Cimetidine did not lessen the ability of the cancer cells to make angiogenic factors (hormone-like agents that activate angiogenesis), so it seemed to be acting directly on endothelial cells. Indeed, clinical concentrations of cimetidine were shown to diminish the capacity of endothelial cells in culture to roll themselves into tubes - a necessary step in the formation of new capillaries. This is likely because of its impact on endothlelial expression of E-selectin [14].

Cimetidine has been in use for a number of years. It is generally well tolerated, and appears to be quite safe. The dose schedule we are using in cancer care is the same as that approved for use in prevention and treatment of ulcers. However, high doses of cimetidine have the potential to increase estrogenic activity by blocking the CYP450 enzyme that metabolizes estrogens. Occasional cases of gynecomastia (inappropriate breast growth) have been reported in males treated with high doses of this drug [15]. For this reason, Oasis of Hope chooses not to use cimetidine in women with estrogen-sensitive breast cancers.

Valproic Acid

Valproic acid is a member of a class of drugs known as "histone deacetylase inhibitors" that have recently shown versatile anti-cancer effects in animal studies. Acetylation, in which chemical structures known as acetyl groups are enzymatically linked to proteins is often required for efficient transcription of genes. Transcription is the process whereby nuclear DNA is used as a template for production of messenger RNA which in turn serves as a template for synthesis of new proteins. Acetylation of DNA-binding proteins known as histones usually aids the transcription of genes. Proteins known as co-activators promote acetylation of histones near specific genes to promote their transcription. However, it is sometimes physiologically desirable to suppress gene transcription, so cells also produce enzymes known as histone deacetylases (HDACs). As their name implies, they remove the acetyl groups from histones and other acetylated proteins.

In many cancers, anomalously decreased transcription of certain genes, known as suppressor genes, contributes to the malignant behavior of cancer. These genes code for proteins that have anti-proliferative effects in the cell. Some years ago, it occurred to cancer scientists that excessive or inappropriate HDAC activity might be responsible for the suppressed transcription of certain suppressor genes. They reasoned that, if this were the case, drugs which inhibit HDACs might boost the transcription of these suppressor genes and thereby make the cancer less aggressive and more controllable. When they treated cancer cells with chemicals that could inhibit HDAC, they were gratified to observe that the cancer cells often decreased their rate of multiplication, were more prone to apoptosis, and were easier to kill with cytotoxic cancer drugs. In some cases, the drugs had a "redifferentiating" effect, meaning that the cancer cells looked and acted more like the healthy tissues from which they were derived. In mice transplanted with human cancers, treatment with HDAC inhibitory drugs slowed cancer growth and increased the efficacy of cytotoxic chemotherapeutic drugs or radiotherapy [16-22].

However, the researchers were surprised to find that increased expression of proteins coded by suppressor genes usually was not clearly responsible for these benefits of HDAC inhibitors. In fact, many proteins inside and outside the nucleus are susceptible to reversible acetylation, and so HDAC inhibitors may be influencing the structure and function of a great number of regulatory cellular proteins by boosting their acetylation. Why HDAC inhibition tends to have such a favorable effect on the behavior of cancer cells remains unclear and is a subject of active investigation. Perhaps one way to look at it is this: the unregulated growth and relative invincibility of cancer cells reflects a carefully balanced regulatory system. Treating with HDAC inhibitors is rather like throwing a monkey wrench into this mechanism, inducing an alteration of cellular behavior. Fortunately, this alteration tends to be positive for the patient. Moreover, HDAC inhibitors tend to be well tolerated, having comparatively little impact on the function or viability of most healthy tissues [23].

Remarkably, HDAC inhibitors also have anti-angiogenic effects, acting directly on endothelial cells to slow the development of new blood vessels required for cancer growth and spread [24-26]. These drugs can also suppress tumor production of certain angiogenic factors, notably vascular endothelial growth factor (VEGF), which are crucial stimulants to tumor angiogenesis [27]. This latter effect is at least partly attributable to decreased activity of a protein (transcription factor) known as hypoxia-inducible factor-1, which promotes the angiogenic process in poorly oxygenated tumors [28,29]. Yet a further benefit is that

HDAC inhibitors can increase cancer cell production of certain membrane proteins that help NK cells and cytotoxic lymphocytes bind to and target cancer cells [30]. So HDAC inhibitors can provide a versatile range of benefits in cancer therapy.

German researchers discovered a few years ago that a time-tested anti-epileptic drug, valproic acid, acts as an HDAC inhibitor in concentrations that can be achieved clinically [31-33]. Furthermore, aside from the fact that valproic acid sometimes produces mild sedation, it is usually quite well tolerated, and thus could be suitable for long-term use in the management of cancer. Experimental studies have confirmed that valproic acid has the cancer retardant and anti-angiogenic effects seen with other HDAC inhibitors [25,31,34-39]. As contrasted with other agents that are being developed as new drugs for HDAC inhibition, valproate has the merit of being currently available, with an acceptable side effect profile that is well known, and it is a relatively inexpensive old drug.

Cancer scientists in Mexico City have already conducted a Phase I study of valproic acid as a cancer drug [40]. This study confirmed that administration of valproic acid in a clinically tolerable dose range was able to increase the acetylation of histone proteins in the majority of patients, showing that this drug does indeed function as an HDAC inhibitor in humans when administered in feasible amounts. We currently use a dose range of 1,500-2,000 mg daily, which is within the range validated in this study.

Hormone Blocking Agents

Some cancers are dependent on specific hormones for optimal growth and survival. For example, many breast cancers require estrogen, and are said to be estrogen-sensitive.

Analogously, many prostate cancers require testosterone to grow and thrive. This is especially true during the earlier stages of the disease. That's why medical science has developed specific drugs that can inhibit the production or activity of these sex hormones, for use in cancer therapy. This strategy has become a standard part of cancer management, with well-documented benefits for controlling cancer spread and prolonging patient survival. So these hormone-blocking drugs are included in the IRT protocols for hormone-dependent breast and prostate cancers. The good news about these agents is that they don't have the range of side-effects that cytotoxic chemotherapies have. The unavoidable bad news about them is that loss of estrogen in women, and of testosterone in men, can have undesirable physiological effects. In particular, men lose sexual potency when deprived of testosterone. Many of our patients with hormone-sensitive prostate cancer choose not to use testosterone-blocking drugs. As is always the case at Oasis of Hope, the patient is the final arbiter regarding the therapy that he or she receives.

With respect to estrogen-sensitive breast cancers, our therapeutic approach depends on whether the woman is pre- or post-menopausal. In pre-menopausal women with estrogen-sensitive breast cancers, we standardly use the drug tamoxifen, which binds to the estrogen receptor in a way that diminishes its growth-promoting activity in breast cancers. Tamoxifen is known as an estrogen antagonist, because it prevents estrogen from binding to the receptors that mediate its hormonal activity. The use of tamoxifen effectively entails the induction of menopause in pre-menopausal women. This is unfortunate. But menopause is part of the natural life cycle in any case, so most women learn to live with this. Tamoxifen is generally considered a safe drug, though its long-term use does increase risk for cancers of the uterine endometrium.

In post-menopausal women, the ovaries are no longer generating estrogens. Nonetheless, a certain amount of estrogen is still produced in fat cells. Fat cells (adipocytes) contain an enzyme called aromatase that can convert circulating androgens to estrogen. Please note that healthy women normally produce very small amounts of "male" hormones. Drugs known as aromatase inhibitors can inhibit this fat-mediated conversion of androgen to estrogen, and so can greatly reduce estrogen levels in post-menopausal women. They don't influence ovarian production of estrogen in pre-menopausal women, and so aren't used in pre-menopausal patients. Studies show that aromatase inhibitors do a better job than tamoxifen for slowing or reversing the spread of estrogen-sensitive breast cancers in post-menopausal women, so this is the option which Oasis of Hope uses in the management of estrogen-sensitive post-menopausal breast cancer [41]. Several different aromatase inhibitors are now available for clinical use – with generic names like "anastrazole" or "letrozole." Since it is not yet clear which of these drugs is clinically superior, our doctors use their own judgment in choosing them. Aside from the fact that these drugs induce a loss of estrogen activity, they are well tolerated.

Years ago, the traditional therapy for testosterone-dependent prostate cancer was a surgery known as "orchiectomy," which is the medical term for castration. Because this was a less than popular option with most patients, pharmaceutical companies have developed drugs that can inhibit the function or production of testosterone, while allowing the patient to keep his testicles. Not surprisingly, this strategy has proved much more popular, and is the approach we recommend at Oasis of Hope.

Two drug-based strategies are commonly used for suppressing testosterone activity in androgen-dependent prostate cancer. One of these is to block the testosterone receptor with a drug such as Casodex, also known as bicalutimide. This approach is quite analogous to the use of tamoxifen in estrogen-sensitive breast cancer. The drug binds to the androgen receptor in a way that inhibits its activity. An alternative approach is to suppress testicular testosterone production with a drug that works on the brain to block its production of a hormone known as luteinizing hormone (LII). LH activity is crucial for efficient testosterone production by the testes. The drugs most commonly used to achieve this are known as luteinizing hormone releasing hormone (LHRH) agonists, because they mimic the activity of LHRH, a brain hormone that stimulates LH release [42]. One would think that such drugs would increase LH release – and in fact they do so temporarily – but prolonged continual use of these drugs actually causes a sustained decrease in LH release, owing to the fact that the brain loses its sensitivity to LHRH stimulation. The LHRH agonist drugs that are currently available are goserelin (Zoladex) and leuprolide (Lupron). They are injected in depot formulations once every several months.

The loss of LH activity associated with the prolonged use of LHRH antagonist drugs causes a temporary atrophy of the testes. The good news is that, after these drugs are discontinued, testosterone production usually returns to normal levels within 18 months [43].

13

Surgery and Radiation Therapy at Oasis of Hope

Localized tumor masses can often be effectively treated by radiotherapy or surgical excision. Such measures are often curative in early stage cancer, and can be used to relieve pain or pressure in patients with more advanced disease. Like other credible cancer clinics, Oasis of Hope uses surgery or radiotherapy when they are warranted. But, unlike most other cancer clinics, we use a variety of adjuvant measures that are intended to make radiotherapy more effective, and surgery less traumatic.

Tumor cells are often hypoxic because the vascular system feeding tumors tends to be haphazard and inefficient. Unfortunately, effective cell killing by radiation requires the presence of molecular oxygen, as this catalyzes the damage to cellular DNA [1]. Thus, hypoxic tumor cells can be less sensitive to radiotherapy than are healthy normal tissues that are well oxygenated. For this reason, Oasis of Hope employs several adjunctive strategies intended to boost tumor oxygen content. The oxygen-transporter Perftec, the anti-inflammatory agent pentoxifylline, and ozone autohemotherapy work in various complementary ways to: increase the oxygen content of the blood; make red and white blood cells more distensible so that blood can flow through tumors more efficiently; and increase the capacity of red blood cells to deliver oxygen to tissues [2-5]. These strategies have a selective impact on the radiosensitivity of hypoxic tumor regions, since increasing the oxygenation of healthy tissues that are already well oxygenated has little impact on the radiation response of healthy tissues. These measures are also used in conjunction with chemotherapy or intravenous vitamin C, since poor oxygenation can make tumor cells less responsive to these therapies as well [6-7].

Pentoxifylline is a safe anti-inflammatory drug that has been in use for decades. Numerous studies in tumor-bearing rodents have shown that administration of tolerable doses of pentoxifylline can boost the oxygen content of tumors and thereby improve the responsiveness of these tumors to radiotherapy [3,4]. Pentoxifylline appears to achieve this by making leukocytes as well as red cells more distensible – an effect similar to that of ozone autohemotherapy – while also lessening the resistance to tumor blood flow by decreasing tumor "interstitial pressure." Since Perftec is currently available only in Mexico and Russia, pentoxifylline may be a good alternative for cancer clinics that Oasis of Hope will open in the future around the world.

Oasis of Hope employs additional strategies to make cancers more sensitive to radiotherapy. Salsalate and silibinin, by suppressing the activation of a cellular factor known as NF-kappaB [8-11], block a key mechanism whereby radiated tumor cells increase their survival [12]. Good vitamin D status, assured through effective vitamin D supplementation, can also improve the radiation responsiveness of some tumors [13-14]. Glutamine, a prominent component of our GPG supplement, has been shown to protect the health of intestinal tissues exposed to radiation [15-16].

With respect to surgery, the comprehensive nutritional support provided to our patients can be expected to promote efficient healing. One of the risks associated with cancer surgery is that the systemic inflammation, immunosuppression, and dislodgement of tumor cells associated with such surgery can increase the risk that new metastases will form in the post-surgical period. Anti-inflammatory agents such as cimetidine and salsalate, as well as immunosupportive nutrients such as melatonin and selenium, are employed by Oasis of Hope in conjunction with surgery, and are intended to minimize the risk that surgery will provoke new metastasis formation [17-22].

When our patients undergo major surgery that entails significant blood loss, we are able to employ a type of "artificial blood," an oxygen-carrying chemical emulsion known as "Perftec" [23]. This ensures that the patient's brain and other vital organs continue to receive adequate oxygenation during the surgery and recovery period, without the need for blood transfusions. Blood transfusions, especially if the blood has been stored for long periods of time, can often trigger inflammatory reactions that can complicate post-surgical recovery, and in some instances can lead to life-threatening multiple organ failure [23]. Perftec, or analogous blood substitutes, are not available in the U.S. or most other countries as of yet. It was registered for commercial medical use in Mexico by the Secretary of Health in November 2005 and is used in Oasis of Hope and other leading medical institutions throughout the nation.

A recent clinical trial, conducted in patients subjected to cardiac surgery with cardiopulmonary bypass, showed that infusion of Perftec emulsion enhanced patient safety during periods of intraoperative anemia, decreased the percentage of patients who required blood transfusion, reduced the units of allogeneic packed red blood cells transfused per patient, and significantly reduced the use of blood derivatives [23].

14
...
Oasis of Hope Diet and Exercise

Throughout most of the twentieth century, age-adjusted death rates for many of our most common cancers were vastly lower in much of the Third World than in comparatively wealthy industrialized countries such as the United States. These types of cancers thus became known as "Western cancers." They include cancers of the breast, prostate, colon, ovary, uterine endometrium, and pancreas – cancers that, along with tobacco-induced lung cancer, constitute the main causes of cancer mortality in the U.S. today.

Why have these cancers been so less common in poorer societies? The most reasonable current explanation seems to be that, in poor societies, blood levels of two key growth factors – insulin and free insulin-like growth factor-I (IGF-I) – tend to be much lower than in wealthier countries [1,2]. Insulin and/or IGF-I stimulate the proliferation of the epithelial tissues from which these cancers arise. They also inhibit the process of apoptosis, which is an important way in which the body gets rid of cells which have sustained mutagenic DNA damage [3]. The combination of increased proliferation – which makes DNA damage more likely – and suppression of the mechanism that rids the body of mutated cells, is a potent stimulus to cancer induction.

What aspects of a Western diet and lifestyle are primarily responsible for our higher levels of insulin and free IGF-I? We speak of "free" IGF-I because there are various proteins in the blood that bind to IGF-I, rendering it inactive. Only the unbound "free" IGF-I can interact with cell receptors. Factors such as abdominal obesity, fatty diets, especially those rich in saturated fats, and sedentary lifestyle are typically associated with increased blood levels of insulin. Under these conditions, skeletal muscle becomes less sensitive to the glucose-transporting activity of insulin. Because of insulin resistance, the body tends to increase the secretion and slow the removal of insulin to compensate for this. This increase in insulin levels tends to increase blood levels of free IGF-I, since insulin acts on the liver to boost IGF-I production while also slowing the production of a binding protein, IGFBP-1, that antagonizes IGF-I's activity [4].

Another lifestyle factor that promotes increased IGF-I levels is a relatively high intake of "high quality" protein. In Third World societies where people eat a mostly plant-based vegan diet, total daily protein intakes tend to be relatively low. The proteins consumed tend to be lower in certain nutritionally essential amino acids, such as methionine, for example, than the "high quality" animal proteins that predominate in Western diets. The relative paucity of certain essential amino acids in vegan diets of moderate protein content can lead to a decrease in the liver's production of IGF-I, and an increase in IGFBP-1 production [5,6]. It's no coincidence that, in rural China, where most people have eaten a quasi-vegan diet for centuries, the provinces with the highest intakes of animal protein are the ones at highest risk for most types of cancer. This has been revealed by the world's most ambitious epidemiological investigation, the China Study [7,8].

These considerations imply that lean people who consume quasi-vegan diets that are low in fat and moderate in protein, and who get regular exercise, can be expected to have relatively low levels of both insulin and free IGF-I, and to enjoy decreased risk for Western cancers. At least until recently, a high proportion of people in Third World societies fit this description.

As noted, the relatively high levels of insulin and free IGF-I characteristic of "advanced" societies can act directly on their target tissues to promote cancer induction. They can also act in indirect ways to boost cancer risk. In particular, this pattern of hormone activity tends to accelerate sexual maturation in girls and increase blood levels of free sex hormones [9,10]. These circumstances are known to increase risk for breast and endometrial cancers. Obesity, per se, increases estrogen levels in postmenopausal women, as fat cells are capable of producing estrogen from other circulating steroid hormones [11].

Of course, at Oasis of Hope we are primarily focused on treating cancer rather than preventing it. What is the relevance of these considerations to cancer treatment? Insulin and/or free IGF-I have growth factor activity for many, though not all, cancers. This growth factor activity makes cancer cells multiply faster, increase their capacity to spread throughout the body, evoke angiogenesis, lessen their rate of spontaneous cell death, and render them less sensitive to elimination by chemotherapy [12]. In other words, if a cancer is sensitive to either insulin or free IGF-I, a patient's prognosis will be better if the insulin and free IGF-I levels are kept relatively low. Admittedly, some cancers aren't responsive to these hormones. Since there aren't any simple inexpensive tests that can determine this, it's prudent to assume that a cancer is responsive to these hormones.

Working with volunteers enrolled in the Pritikin diet-exercise program, Dr. James Barnard and colleagues of UCLA have done some studies that beautifully illustrate these points [13,14]. They took serum samples from patients who were about to enroll in the program, and then took serum from the same patients after they had been on the program for 3 weeks. They also obtained serum from people who had followed the Pritikin Program for a number of years. To clarify, the Pritikin Program requires people to eat an unrefined quasi-vegan diet, very low in total fat, moderate in protein, and high in carbohydrate, while engaging in regular aerobic exercise. People who are overweight typically lose weight rapidly, a factor that contributes to the impact of this program on insulin sensitivity. As expected, Dr. Barnard was able to confirm that, after only 3 weeks, this regimen was associated with rather substantial reductions in blood levels of both insulin and free IGF-I.

These researchers then took human prostate cancer cell lines and incubated them in the various serums obtained from the Pritikin patients and the long-term Pritikin devotees. They observed that the cancer cells grew more slowly, and were more prone to apoptotic cell death, when incubated in the post-Pritikin serum (the serum obtained after 3 weeks of the program) than when incubated in the pre-Pritikin serum. The serum from long-term Pritikinists was even less supportive of cancer cells growth. The cancer cells grew 44% more slowly, and had a manifold higher rate of spontaneous cell death as contrasted to cells grown in pre-Pritikin serum. More recent studies with breast cancer cell lines have yielded similar though less dramatic findings [15].

Meanwhile, Dr. Dean Ornish has been conducting a remarkable study with volunteers who are in the early stages of prostate cancer [16]. Volunteers were randomized either to participate in a special diet-lifestyle program or to receive standard care. The program consists of a very-low-fat (about 10% fat calories), wholly vegan diet, emphasizing whole foods, complemented by regular aerobic exercise and stress control training. This program is rather like a more stringently vegan version of the Pritikin Program. Ornish is following the clinical progress of these patients by monitoring their PSA levels. During the first year, PSA decreased on average by 4% by those enrolled in this lifestyle program, while on average it rose 6% in the control group. Furthermore, as in Barnard's Pritikin studies, a prostate cancer cell line grew much less rapidly in serum obtained from patients enrolled in the lifestyle program, as compared to serum obtained from the patients serving as controls.

Of related interest are recent studies in women with breast cancer. Those with relatively high insulin levels have a decidedly poorer prognosis than those with relatively low insulin levels [17,18]. In patients with either breast or colorectal cancer, significant aerobic exercise training – equivalent to brisk walking for a half-hour a day – has been linked to improved prognosis. This is hardly surprising since exercise tends to improve insulin sensitivity. The effect was substantial as optimal levels of exercise were associated with reductions in risk of cancer mortality of 50% or more [19-21]. Studies also demonstrate that exercise training prior to and during cancer chemotherapy may have a favorable impact on immune function, tends to offset the fatigue often associated with such therapy, and may have other favorable effects on perceived quality of life [22,23].

We thus have strong reason to suspect that lifestyle factors can have a major impact on survival in prostate, breast, and colorectal cancers. Not unlikely, comparable findings will be established with respect to certain other cancers as well once the pertinent studies are conducted.

Oasis of Hope thus recommends its cancer patients to modify their lifestyles in ways that will reduce their blood levels of insulin and free IGF-I. This recommendation is of particular importance for patients with breast, colorectal, or prostate cancer. It may be prudent for patients with other types of cancer to heed this advice as well.

Ideally, it is desirable for patients to adopt a 100% plant-based diet. The exception is fish oil capsules, which will not have a negative impact on insulin sensitivity. This diet is low in total fats (under 15% of calories) and moderate in protein. Bean and soy consumption should be moderate as well. Since high-glycemic-index carbohydrates can markedly boost post-meal insulin levels, it may be advisable to emphasize whole-food carbohydrate sources that are relatively low in glycemic index. This includes pastas, most whole fruits, and whole-grain products that are relatively structurally intact. For example, sprouted wheat breads as compared to wheat flour breads.

This dietary program should be complemented by regular aerobic exercise. Exercise where the patient supports his/her own weight, such as brisk walking, stair-climbing, elliptical gliders, or treadmills, is preferable. For patients less than ideally thin, Oasis of Hope has a very effective regimen for fat loss. The Oasis of Hope Leanness Program is based on a "mini-fast with exercise" strategy developed by Austrian physician Dr. Babak Bahadori [24]. When volunteers from the hospital staff tried this program on themselves, the participants on average lost one-quarter of their initial body fat. The best thing about this program is that it is sustainable for life, and does not require calorie counting or carb avoidance.

For patients that are unwilling to adopt a fully vegan diet, a more modest benefit can result by adopting a "Mediterranean" diet in conjunction with regular exercise. The "Mediterranean" approach to eating discourages the consumption of red meat and fatty dairy products, allows moderate amounts of lean white meat or fish, and emphasizes large intakes of fruits, vegetables (often sautéed in olive oil), beans, and whole grains. This approach tends to improve insulin sensitivity because it minimizes intakes of saturated fat while often increasing those of unsaturated fat. A low ratio of saturated to unsaturated fats tends to improve insulin sensitivity [25]. This strategy probably won't lower free IGF-I or boost insulin sensitivity as effectively as a low-fat vegan diet, but it is likely to be protective relative to the fatty meat-based diets favored by most Americans.

The Mediterranean dietary tradition encourages moderated consumption of wine with meals. In fact, there is some evidence that moderate regular alcohol consumption (beer or liquors count too, not just wine) can have a favorable influence on insulin sensitivity [26], is associated with slightly lower free IGF-I levels [27,28], and may even increase life expectancy [29,30]. So there doesn't seem to be any good reason why cancer patients should abstain from alcohol if consumption stays in a healthful range. Excessive alcohol intake can degrade insulin sensitivity and create many health risks. For men, that means no more than three drinks a day. Since women absorb alcohol more efficiently, they should consume no more than two drinks a day.

Are there any foods that may be specifically beneficial to cancer patients? Certain vegetables – notably cruciferous vegetables (cabbage, broccoli, cauliflower, kale, etc.) and allium vegetables (onions and garlic) contain compounds that induce a so-called phase II response. That is, they cause the body's cells to make higher levels of various antioxidants as well as enzymes which assist in the detoxification of carcinogens and drugs [31,32]. Theoretically, this could make healthy normal tissues more resilient when they have to cope with cytotoxic chemotherapeutic drugs or radiotherapy. Whether this strategy could be of real practical importance to patients undergoing chemotherapy is not yet clear. In any case, such foods might reduce risk for developing additional cancers, and they certainly won't harm the overall health of a person.

Another food with particular promise for cancer patients may be spirulina. Very recent research shows that spirulina contains high amounts of a phytonutrient known as "phycocyanobilin"

(PCB for short – not to be confused with the polychlorinated biphenyls that are environmental hazards) that can act as a potent inhibitor of the chief source of excess oxidant stress in the body, the enzyme complex NADPH oxidase [33,34]. There is growing evidence that NADPH oxidase is activated in many cancers, and this activity tends to boost the proliferation and spread of cancer cells while protecting them from apoptotic cell death [35-37]. Moreover, NADPH oxidase activity in endothelial cells is now known to play a key role in the process of angiogenesis [38,39]. Thus, there is good reason to suspect that partial inhibition of NADPH oxidase may help to slow the spread of certain cancers, both by direct effects on cancer cells and by an anti-angiogenic effect. Oral administration of spirulina in rodents has anti-inflammatory effects that probably are attributable to inhibition of NADPH oxidase. It seems likely that suitably high intakes of spirulina would have a comparable impact in humans.

A further potential advantage of spirulina for cancer patients is that it contains polysaccharides that have immunostimulant activity when administered orally. This might boost the ability of natural killer cells or cytotoxic T lymphocytes to slow or prevent the metastatic spread of a cancer [40]. Thus, until more relevant data is available, it is prudent for cancer patients to take up to two heaping tablespoons of spirulina daily (one twice daily). Spirulina is most palatable when incorporated into smoothies featuring such ingredients as fruit juice, soy milk, and bananas or other whole fruit.

The Oasis of Hope Kitchen

Virtually anyone who has had the opportunity to dine at the Oasis of Hope could testify that the food served is one of the highlights of the overall experience. Though the doctors, nurses and medical scientists do their best for the patients, the true genius of the Oasis of Hope kitchen staff must be acknowledged. The food served at Oasis of Hope is consistent with its dietary principles. Everything is either vegan, or contains modest amounts of fish, chicken, or eggs, in the Mediterranean style. Whole grains are emphasized, fruits, fresh juices, beans, vegetables, and soups are available in profusion, and the dishes are almost always low in fat and salt. This may sound a bit spartan – but in fact the food is invariably delicious. The dining experience at Oasis of Hope teaches that it is feasible to eat a diet that promotes optimal health while providing real culinary pleasure at the same time. Our intent is that patients will take this insight home with them, and will continue eating healthfully in the way they have learned at Oasis of Hope.

Meal times are not just about food; they are also an occasion for friendship, camaraderie, and laughter. In the dining commons, patient and staff interact; it is often difficult to tell who the patients are because they are encouraged to dress in comfortable clothing verses the typical hospital gown that often leaves much to be desired. It is frequent to see diners continuing to receive i.v. infusions of chemotherapy or vitamin C while they enjoy the delicious food. Meals are an excellent chance for patients to get to know each other better, and to share their experiences coping with cancer. It is heartwarming to see how often laughter breaks out, as diners exchange jokes and amusing anecdotes. For the patients, dining at Oasis of Hope not only nourishes the body, but also contributes to promoting their emotional and spiritual well being – it's a key part of the healing experience.

111

15

. . .

Emotional Support at Oasis of Hope

What if a person facing cancer was forced to decide between being cared for by a doctor or a counselor? Whom would he/she choose? Most people recognize that speaking with a counselor would be helpful – but not at the cost of not being able to see their doctor. A person might be thought crazy if he chose to see a psychologist instead of the oncologist. In most hospitals, patients do not encounter this dilemma. The choice has already been made. It is rare to find counseling provided in cancer treatment centers. At best, there may be a social worker who comes for a quick interview. Notes are entered into the medical file and that is it. Two years ago, the Oasis of Hope director of counseling attended the annual convention of the Association of Oncology Social Workers. The director came back very excited about working at Oasis of Hope, explaining during breaks at the conference, other social workers would ask about the program at Oasis of Hope. They all were amazed that Oasis of Hope truly integrates emotional support into its treatment program, and they stated that they could only dream of working in such a place. In most cancer treatment centers, emotional support is a nice thought that happens minimally if at all.

This is not the case at Oasis of Hope. Counseling is an integral part of the treatment program. Why? Cancer, its symptoms, and treatments, will tax the strongest of people. Fear, anxiety, anger and other strong emotions are promoted by cancer, and few people have had to deal with such a difficult situation that stresses them in so many different ways at the same time. The whole experience can affect a person's sense of self, employment, energy level, sexuality, interpersonal relationships, hopes and dreams, hobbies, and faith. All of these issues, if not managed adequately, can have a negative influence on the treatment outcome of a patient. In fact, depression is fairly common in cancer patients, and this is quite understandable [1].

More than 2000 years ago, the Greeks recognized instinctively that health and emotions always came together. For Hippocrates, the father of medicine, some factors were essential to achieving health, like a healthy diet, pure water, exercise, and support of family and friends. But essential too were the emotions, as well as relaxing activities that soothed them [2].

The Oasis of Hope approach likewise emphasizes the connection between the emotions and physical outcome. An individual's constitution at birth, which is mainly genetically determined, and his/her coping skills, which depend largely on personality, can lead to the development of disease later in life [3,4]. Some decades ago, scientists began to define the ways in which emotional distress can affect our immunity and predispose us to certain illnesses such as cancer [5].

Beginning back in the 1950's, L. LeShan [4,6] dedicated decades to studying and reviewing the literature on this matter, and concluded that there were four key types of personality characteristics that tended to lead to the beginning of malignancy in cancer patients [7]:

1. The loss of an important emotional relationship
2. An inability to express anger or resentment
3. An unusual amount of self-dislike and distress
4. Feelings of hopelessness and helplessness

Furthermore, chronic stress affects the body negatively in several other ways. Through imbalance of the autonomic nervous system, it affects the rhythm of the beats of the heart, and may induce abnormal cell division that could potentially promote cancer [8]. Also, stress might be able to impair the body's defenses against cancer by altering the molecular mechanisms responsible for repairing faulty DNA in cells [9].

At Oasis of Hope, there are a number of counselors on staff to help patients learn how to manage the stress of cancer, and to help them transition from a feeling of hopelessness to a feeling of empowerment. The counselors help patients experience and work through the normal emotional stages of a cancer crisis.

The first stage experienced by most people is shock. Imagine being blind-sided so unexpectedly and hard that you had no clue what hit you? That is exactly the feeling that overwhelms a person when a doctor states, "We found cancer." When a person is in shock, family, friends and a support team are critical.

The next stage is denial. Think of a child falling down hard on the playground during P.E. and hearing the other kids gasp, "ooooohhhh." The natural instinct is to pop right up and declare, "I'm okay!" only to look down and see the bloody knee. Then, the delayed tears would come. When a patient is diagnosed, he may wish to bounce right back stating, "I'm okay, I'm going to be okay." He may state, "Those doctors are wrong, I am going to get a second opinion." He may have even waited days or weeks until he was willing to share the news with loved ones. This is normal.

Fear is the third emotional stage. A flurry of questions and doubts begin to race through when reality sets in. All the unknowns create strong emotions of fear and anxiety. Patients often contemplate many unsettling questions such as, "Am I going to die? Am I going to have lots of pain? Will I suffer much from the treatments? If I die, who is going to take care of my children?" The natural tendency is to keep these fears private. The unnatural thing to do is to externalize and address fears. The healthy thing to do is to share with others exactly what is being experienced.

Grief is a normal part of experiencing a diagnosis of cancer and the ensuing treatment. Few people realize how many feelings of loss a patient goes through. The seeming loss of hopes and dreams for the future can bring on grief. The loss of a normal routine can feel devastating. A person should not go through this process alone.

Feelings of loss are normally followed by the fifth stage, which is anger. Think of a child who has his toy snatched away from him by a bully. At first, he doesn't know what happened. Then, he can't believe it. His fear of the bully is paralyzing and then he starts to cry. After a time of crying, he gets angry. It is common for a patient to express anger and frustration.

Anger is followed by a stage of guilt. Questions of "Why me?" and "What did I do to deserve this?" are common. With the help of Oasis of Hope counselors, the feelings of anger and grief can be transformed into the seventh stage, which is acceptance and resolve. When a patient is able to accept the situation, she is emotionally ready to hope and believe that healing is possible, and then can find the courage to take action, knowing all the time that the treatment outcome may not be what is desired.

Sarah Mahoney authored a great guideline for what to do when diagnosed with cancer entitled "This is Your Brain On Illness" [10]. In her article, Mahoney acknowledges the emotional stages that a cancer patient experiences, and she specifies actions that can be taken to manage the stress and make effective treatment decisions. Her main points are: 1) The first 5 minutes: You're in shock, just take it all in; 2) The first 24 hours: You seize control. Don't commit to treatment yet; 3) The first week: You hit a slump; 4) Identify your feelings; 5) Recruit your "A" team; 6) Investigate "self-management" programs; 7) Embrace your inner grouch; 8) Resist redefining yourself.

There is a close link between the experience of mind and the physiological performance of the body [11]. The body is equipped with psychological and biological mechanisms that allow the brain and immune system to communicate with each other. Physical function and the way a person thinks, reacts, copes, and perceives emotions, are all connected and influence each other.

All cognitions, feelings and emotions are chemical. They influence the biochemistry and physiology of a person at the cellular level. They can produce changes within the endocrine and immune systems in diverse ways, including modulation of specialized nerve pathways and chemical messengers [11]. The renowned pathologist David Felton first discovered that the spleen contains nerve fibers that are intimately associated with the cells of the immune system, such as lymphocytes and natural killer cells. Both the nerve endings and the immune cells produce similar message molecules, such as neuropeptides, referred to by Candace Pert in her book as the Molecules of Emotion [12]. Norman Cousins, the great scholar and humanitarian, confirmed this concept in his book *Head First: The Biology of Hope* [13] with this statement, "The human mind converts ideas and expectations into biochemical realities."

The Oasis of Hope counselors have the insight that when negative emotions and stressors are managed adequately, the patient can leverage his/her emotional energy toward healing. One of the most effective ways to help a patient transition from fear and anxiety to hope and faith is by helping him/her build a social support system. This is unnatural at first. The tendency for people in crisis is to withdraw socially. But isolation increases emotional distress. Activities that facilitate communication and social interaction help decrease a patient's anxiety and stress levels. Story telling [14], group therapy, and even cancer support groups through video conferencing [15] are all effective at improving a patient's outlook. The main point is that cancer is not a journey that should be taken alone. To successfully navigate all of the roadblocks, pitfalls, and sinkholes of cancer, one must reach out to others.

The attitude and will that a patient has can have a big impact on whether or not health will be recovered. At Oasis of Hope patients are active partners in all stages of treatment, rather than passive recipients of medical intervention. By becoming actively involved in a self-healing process, patients can shift from the feelings of helplessness and hopelessness that increase the impairment of the immune system, to a sense of control. There is evidence that being empowered with knowledge and being part of the decision-making process results in an improved health outcome; whereas passivity and apparent lack of control may be harmful to health [16]. The Oasis of Hope Emotional Support Team helps each patient participate in her own healing process, develop a passionate involvement with life, and find a unique purpose and meaning in illness and in health. This is the principle reason why Oasis of Hope has not reduced emotional support to a single visit from a social worker for a quick assessment. The counseling program has daily activities and is a full part of the treatment program.

Through education sessions, group therapy, individual counseling, laughter therapy, and music and art programs, the counselors at Oasis of Hope support patients as they transform a paradigm of helplessness to a new hope-filled outlook. Patients learn the advantages of taking care of the physical, emotional, and spiritual aspects of their lives. Counselors motivate patients and companions to make positive changes in their thinking style by helping them to understand the big impact that the mind has on health.

If a shift from a perception that a person is dying from cancer can be made toward a renewed sense that a person is living with cancer, much of the emotional distress and burdens are alleviated. People need permission to engage in life and enjoy each day whether cancer is present or not. The essence of the Oasis of Hope emotional support program is just that. It is an invitation to live each day to the fullest.

16

...

Caring for the Spirit at Oasis of Hope

Patients at Oasis of Hope in the 1960s through the early 2000s, would daily witness a kind old gentleman in a doctor's coat getting out of his burgundy Mercury Grand Marquis and pulling out his briefcase and guitar case from the trunk. As aged and frail as he was, his heart-felt smile and greeting brought strength to anyone who was so fortunate to have met him. Dr. Ernesto Contreras, Sr., founder of the Oasis of Hope, had been providing his unique blend of scientific medicine and healing art to the patients at the hospital for more than 35 years.

Dr. Contreras, Sr. would see patients in his consultation office in the mornings to go over lab work and explain medical treatments. In the afternoons, he would get together with all of his patients for fellowship. He would take his guitar and a joke book. Often his jokes were stale but he would laugh so hard and sincerely that everyone would join in the fun. When it came time to sing, he would pull out his songbook. When he realized he couldn't read the small type, he would borrow glasses from the person closest to him. Often, a woman named Peggy would lend her oversized pink framed glasses to Dr. Contreras. He may not have sung like Elton John, but some of the glasses he would borrow could have come right out of Sir Elton John's private collection.

He loved to share incredible facts such as ironic doctor's names he came across including the pediatrician named Dr. Kidd, the radiotherapist named Dr. Burns, and the cardiologist named Dr. Hart. What was remarkable was to see smiles come across the faces of many people in the room who were facing the difficult reality of cancer.

Many of his songs were comical as well. He would take lyrics penned by his patients and sing them to the tune of popular folk songs. Imagine singing to the tune of "Deep In The Heart of Texas" words like, "The Contreras diet, you better best try it (clap, clap, clap, clap), deep in the heart of Oasis." The enzymes too, you need a few (clap, clap, clap, clap), deep in the heart of Oasis. As he would have his patients sing along with him, more smiles would brighten and an occasional tear of relief would be shed. When a patient was discharged, Dr. Contreras would sing his "Farewell" song to send him off with a blessing and love until the next time they would meet.

After jokes and songs, he would ask everyone to form a circle, hold hands and pray. He would pray in a very low and humble voice. He had a simple faith that was contagious. To close, he would prescribe 12 hugs and more tears of relief and joy would often come to the eyes of many.

This story is more than heartwarming; it is fundamental for the treatment approach at Oasis of Hope. Though there were no published clinical trials on the healing importance of a patient's spirituality when Dr. Contreras, Sr. opened Oasis of Hope in 1963, intuitively, he knew that he must address the needs of the whole person — body, mind and spirit. It was because of Dr. Contreras, Sr.'s vision of lifting a patient's spirit that he would integrate music, laughter, prayer and hugs into his medical program. This integration of spiritual support continues to be a hallmark of the Oasis of Hope total care approach - a 45 - year healing legacy.

As scientists, we do not fully understand how the spirituality of a patient impacts his or her health. A number of clinical studies are beginning to skim the surface of this intriguing subject. One explanation of how the spirit of a person can impact her physical health could include the linear relationship between the spirit, mind and body. If there were one word to sum up this linear relationship, it would be psychoneuroendocrinology.

Imagine that a person receives a diagnosis of cancer. This person may be riddled with fear and anxiety related to death, symptoms, and treatment. If the patient had faith that God was going to help, no matter what the outcome would be, this faith would generate positive emotions of peace and maybe even joy. When these emotions were transferred from the soul of the person to the brain, the brain would send signals to the endocrine system that would then produce chemicals that could bring relief from pain and a sense of well-being to the patient.

Another patient with no faith may feel hopeless. This would generate negative emotions that would arrive to the brain. When distress signals are received by the brain, orders are fired out to the endocrine system to produce chemicals such as adrenaline and cortisol to help the patient fight or flee from the perceived danger. These chemicals are helpful in short bursts but when a patient is distressed over a long period of time, the chemicals begin to depress the immune system. A depressed immune system will not help a patient heal.

The interconnection of a person's body, mind and spirit is really not linear at all. It is more like overlapping circles. But it is easy to see how the spirit can affect the emotions that in turn stimulate a physiological response. There are many studies that confirm that a patient's spirituality can ease psychological stress. Patients report that spirituality is an excellent way of coping [1]. Patients have indicated that sharing prayer and religious expression has been effective at lowering emotional distress even when it is done through online chat rooms [2].

Because Oasis of Hope goes beyond cancer eradication to concentrate on the quality of life the patient experiences, spiritual support is emphasized. Clinical studies confirm that religious coping has a positive impact and improves the quality of life in cancer patients [3].

In one study with 27 breast cancer patients, 26 out of the 27 stated that spiritual faith could help cancer patients recuperate, citing prayer, dependence on God, and social support from the faith community as being effective [4]. Another study with 84 patients concluded that helping a patient find meaning in life through spirituality had a positive impact on a patient's ability to manage the emotional strain of cancer [5].

Whether a person professes a belief in God or not, everyone has spiritual needs. In cancer patients, some of the top spiritual needs include: time to think; hope; dealing with unresolved issues; preparation for death; expression of true feelings without being judged; and the opportunity to speak about important relationships [6]. Such needs should not be overlooked. In most hospitals, a visit by a chaplain may happen or it may not. Some families may call a local pastor to come and visit. Usually a time of sharing followed by prayer will happen in these cases and the patient and family members often feel supported. At Oasis of Hope, spiritual support is not an optional accessory. Spiritual health and needs are acknowledged and addressed to the extent that a patient is open to the opportunities from devotions, praise and worship, and prayer times.

Clinical trials confirm the importance of faith, prayer, religious expression, and shared faith. Dr. Contreras, Sr. envisioned an Oasis of Hope with spiritual healing. Today, the spiritual support program thrives as patients become active participants in their healing and the healing of others.

A missionary who provides spiritual counseling at Oasis of Hope recounts some of his experiences:

This is a story of a woman who came to Oasis of Hope as a patient. Even before she came, she recognized that she had a need to get rid of any "baggage" that she might have from her past in order for a complete healing. After a few days at Oasis of Hope, during one of the morning devotions, she burst out and talked about the hurts of her past and how they had affected her whole life and she did not know how to forgive. Our Spiritual Support Team came together and talked with her and offered comfort and prayer. It was during that time that she was able to release those hurts and feel God's love for her in a tangible way. A year later she still attributes her healing to this moment knowing that what she would do medically would work because she had laid down that burden.

Another story tells us about a patient who came through the Oasis of Hope program for three consecutive treatments. At the end of her treatment, she was given a report of being cancer free — a report that many people hope to hear. She broke down crying and came to the spiritual team one day. She couldn't be happy about her good report. She was sure the cancer would come back if she did not change how she felt about her husband. Our team prayed with her, so that she would let go of the things of the past.

17

...

Oasis of Hope IRT Survival Statistics

Though the scientific basis for the IRT protocols have been substantiated in this book, for many, it all comes down to survival statistics. Recently, we analyzed the survival of the first group of patients who have been treated with our relatively new IRT-Q and IRT-C protocols. Because these protocols have been in place for only several years, we obviously have not been able to calculate 5-year survivals yet, but we have been able to determine meaningful 1- and 2-year survivals for the most common types of cancer treated with the IRT-Q protocol. For the current IRT-C protocol, which has now been in use for a little under 2 years, we have had enough experience to calculate 1-year survivals in breast, lung, and colorectal cancer. Since most patients who come to Oasis of Hope have advanced metastatic disease when they get here, we have restricted this analysis to patients who were stage IV at the time of diagnosis, so that our results can be compared objectively with those of other medical centers. Stage IV usually means that metastases are present in distant organs. Also, we have included only those patients who were sufficiently healthy to complete at least 3 courses of therapy, which usually takes about 3 months. In patients diagnosed with stage IV breast cancer, we have also done a separate analysis for those patients who arrived at Oasis of Hope within 6 months of their diagnosis. For many of these patients, Oasis of Hope was their first treatment option.

Tables I and II display our results. The results of "conventional treatment" which we have included for comparison are derived from the National Cancer Institute's recent (2007)

SEER Survival Monograph – "Cancer Survival Among Adults – U.S. SEER Program, 1988-2001." This publication provides average cancer survival rates in major regions of the United States. Unfortunately, this volume does not provide 2-year survivals rates for colorectal cancer, so in this case we have used the 2-year survival results of a major medical center in Toronto. The results seem reasonably concordant with the 1-year results published in the SEER monograph.

Table I. Survival Rates for Stage IV Cancer IRT-Q

Type of Cancer	Oasis IRT-Q		Conventional Treatment *	
	1-Year Survival (%)	2-Year Survival (%)	1-Year Survival (%)	2-Year Survival (%)
Breast	92	68.2	65	44
Breast**	100	88.3	65	44
Lung	76.2	41.2	20	8
Ovarian	95	76.4	62	43
Colorectal	63	42.3	43	29

*National Cancer Institute: U.S. SEER survival monograph 2007
**Patients in whom Oasis of Hope was the 1st treatment options

It is clear that, in terms of survival, Oasis of Hope patients are doing better than those receiving the average standard of care in the U.S. In particular, survival in lung cancer is strikingly better. We are not doing as well with colorectal cancer. This cancer is typically resistant to available chemotherapies. But, even here our results appear to be superior to conventional treatment. Note also that our results with stage IV breast cancer patients who came to Oasis soon after diagnosis are quite good – a doubling of two-year survival relative to conventional therapy.

With respect to the admittedly preliminary results of the IRT-C protocol, it is encouraging that, even without chemotherapy treatments, our patients have been doing better than those on conventional therapy.

Admittedly, we can't claim that many of these patients have been "cured" – in the sense that the cancer has been eliminated and won't come back. But it does seem that we are making some progress toward the goal of turning advanced cancer into a chronic disease that can be managed in the long term – rather like diabetes – as opposed to a rapid death sentence. And remember that our IRT protocols are in a constant state of evolution – barely a month goes by that we don't add some new element to our regimens, or modify them in a way that seems likely to improve their efficacy. So we are cautiously optimistic that we are on the right track, and that our results will continue to improve over the coming years.

Table II. Survival Rates for Stage IV Cancer IRT-C

Type of Cancer	Oasis IRT-C 1-Year Survival (%)	Conventional Treatment* 1-Year Survival (%)
Breast	74.4	65
Breast**	86.7	65
Lung	69	20
Colorectal	76.4	43

*National Cancer Institute: U.S. SEER survival monograph 2007
**Patients in whom Oasis of Hope was the 1st treatment option

These results are promising and suggest that Oasis of Hope should continue to evaluate new therapies and find ways to integrate new proven modalities into a comprehensive cancer management program that can improve the prognosis of a patient, his quality of life, and his ability to engage in normal activities. This is the commitment of the members of the Oasis of Hope Health Group.

Epilogue

■ ■ ■

Uncertainty complicates any and all endeavors; acquiesce to it, and failure is assured. The innumerable variables cancer poses makes it a formidable foe. Those that remain static in their quest to conquer it are doomed, be they researchers, oncologists, or patients. Every advance in the knowledge of cancer's intricate biology brings along a new set of uncertainties; but new opportunities also arise.

No one can deny the success that basic research has brought about in the last three decades. Billions of dollars have been granted to hundreds of thousands of scientists who have gained fame in the prestigious world of cancer research, over 1.5 million scientific publications attest to their relentless work worldwide.

It is largely due to the constant stream of new information coming from this research that has made it possible for the Oasis of Hope Clinical Research Organization to develop and improve its Integrative Regulatory Therapies. Whether some of the research of the various institutes and companies has been profit driven or not, the reality is that we are able to take much of this information and provide benefit to our patients.

I'm proud of the percentage of patients we have been able to help survive cancer in the history of our institution. As we advance and modify our therapies, many have advised that I should not change our proven approach. But the patients that we could not help are a constant reminder that the good is the enemy of the excellent. Not everything that is new is better and not everything that is old is outdated. A balance of the innovative with the time-tested is the premise of our forward approach to a dynamic development of new therapies.

In the ideal world, researchers, clinicians, and investors should be working together to develop therapies that are successful, well tolerated by the patients, easy to apply, and affordable. Though this point of view may categorize me as an idealist, I persist in the quest to develop effective and efficient therapies. I'm proud, blessed, and extremely grateful for the enormously talented team that has joined the Oasis of Hope to envision and seek the impossible dream of alleviating the world of cancer.

Francisco Contreras, MD
Chairman & President
Oasis of Hope Health Group

References

■ ■ ■

Chapter Five- Oxidizing Cancer to Death

1. Sun Y. Free radicals, antioxidant enzymes, and carcinogenesis. Free Radic Biol Med 1990;8(6):583-99.

2. Kwei KA, Finch JS, Thompson EJ, Bowden GT. Transcriptional repression of catalase in mouse skin tumor progression. Neoplasia 2004 September;6(5):440-8.

3. Tas F, Hansel H, Belce A, Ilvan S, Argon A, Camlica H, Topuz E. Oxidative stress in breast cancer. Med Oncol 2005;22(1):11-5.

4. Arnold RS, Shi J, Murad E, Whalen AM, Sun CQ, Polavarapu R, Parthasarathy S, Petros JA, Lambeth JD. Hydrogen peroxide mediates the cell growth and transformation caused by the mitogenic oxidase Nox1. Proc Natl Acad Sci USA 2001 May 8;98(10):5550-5.

5. Vaquero EC, Edderkaoui M, Pandol SJ, Gukovsky I, Gukovskaya AS. Reactive oxygen species produced by NAD(P)H oxidase inhibit apoptosis in pancreatic cancer cells. J Biol Chem2004August.13;279(33):34643-54.

6. Lim SD, Sun C, Lambeth JD, Marshall F, Amin M, Chung L, Petros JA, Arnold RS. Increased Nox1 and hydrogen peroxide in prostate cancer. Prostate 2005 February 1;62(2):200-7.

7. Arnold RS, Shi J, Murad E, Whalen AM, Sun CQ, Polavarapu R, Parthasarathy S, Petros JA, Lambeth JD. Hydrogen peroxide mediates the cell growth and transformation caused by the mitogenic oxidase Nox1. Proc Natl Acad Sci USA 2001 May 8;98(10):5550-5.

8. Chen Q, Espey MG, Krishna MC, Mitchell JB, Corpe CP, Buettner GR, Shacter E, Levine M. Pharmacologic ascorbic acid concentrations selectively kill cancer cells: action as a pro-drug to deliver hydrogen peroxide to tissues. Proc Natl Acad Sci USA 2005September20;102(38):13604-9.

9. Chen Q, Espey MG, Sun AY, Lee JH, Krishna MC, Shacter E, Choyke PL, Pooput C, Kirk KL, Buettner GR, Levine M. Ascorbate in pharmacologic concentrations selectively generates ascorbate radical and hydrogen peroxide in extracellular fluid in vivo. Proc Natl Acad Sci USA 2007 May 22;104(21):8749-54.

10. Padayatty SJ, Sun H, Wang Y, Riordan HD, Hewitt SM, Katz A, Wesley RA, Levine M. Vitamin C pharmacokinetics: implications for oral and intravenous use. Ann Intern Med 2004,April6;140(7):533-7.

11. Padayatty SJ, Levine M. Reevaluation of ascorbate in cancer treatment: emerging evidence, open minds and serendipity. J Am Coll Nutr 2000 August;19(4):423-5.

12. Riordan HD, Casciari JJ, Gonzalez MJ, Riordan NH, Miranda-Massari JR, Taylor P, Jackson JA. A pilot clinical study of continuous intravenous ascorbate in terminal cancer patients. P R Health Sci J 2005 December;24(4):269-76.

13. Padayatty SJ, Riordan HD, Hewitt SM, Katz A, Hoffer LJ, Levine M. Intravenously administered vitamin C as cancer therapy: three cases. CMAJ 2006 March 28;174(7):937-42.

14. Calderon PB, Cadrobbi J, Marques C, Hong-Ngoc N, Jamison JM, Gilloteaux J, Summers JL, Taper HS. Potential therapeutic application of the association of vitamins C and K3 in cancer treatment. Curr Med Chem 2002 December;9(24):2271-85.

15. Sharma RK, Marwaha N, Kumar P, Narang A. Effect of oral water soluble vitamin K on PIVKA-II levels in newborns. Indian Pediatr 1995 August;32(8):863-7.

16. Venugopal M, Jamison JM, Gilloteaux J, Koch JA, Summers M, Giammar D, Sowick C, Summers JL. Synergistic antitumor activity of vitamins C and K3 on human urologic tumor cell lines. Life Sci 1996;59 (17):1389-400.

17. Gilloteaux J, Jamison JM, Neal DR, Summers JL. Cell death by autoschizis in TRAMP prostate carcinoma cells as a result of treatment by ascorbate: menadione combination.UltrastructPathol2005 May;29(3-4):221-35.

18. Zhang W, Negoro T, Satoh K, Jiang Y, Hashimoto K, Kikuchi H, Nishikawa H, Miyata T, Yamamoto Y, Nakano K, Yasumoto E, Nakayachi T, Mineno K, Satoh T, Sakagami H. Synergistic cytotoxic action of vitamin C and vitamin K3. Anticancer Res 2001 September; 21(5):3439-44.

19. Verrax J, Cadrobbi J, Delvaux M, Jamison JM, Gilloteaux J, Summers JL, Taper HS, Buc CP. The association of vitamins C and K3 kills cancer cells mainly by autoschizis, a novel form of cell death. Basis for their potential use as coadjuvants in anticancer therapy. Eur J Med Chem2003May;38(5):451-7.

20. Gilloteaux J, Jamison JM, Arnold D, Neal DR, Summers JL. Morphology and DNA degeneration during autoschizic cell death in bladder carcinoma T24 cells induced by ascorbate and menadione treatment. Anat Rec A Discov Mol Cell Evol Biol 2006 January;

21. McCarty MF, Barroso-Aranda J, Contreras F. A two-phase strategy for treatment of oxidant-dependent cancers. Med Hypotheses 2007;69(3):489-96.

22. Verrax J, Stockis J, Tison A, Taper HS, Calderon PB. Oxidative stress by ascorbate/ menadione association kills K562 human chronic myelogenous leukaemia cells and inhibits its tumour growth in nude mice. Biochem Pharmacol 2006 September 14;72(6):671-80.

23. Taper HS, Jamison JM, Gilloteaux J, Summers JL, Calderon PB. Inhibition of the development of metastases by dietary vitamin C:K3 combination. Life Sci 2004 July 9;75(8):955-67.

24. De LW, Janssens J, Bonte J, Taper HS. Effects of sodium ascorbate (vitamin C) and 2-methyl-1,4-naphthoquinone (vitamin K3) treatment on human tumor cell growth in vitro. II. Synergism with combined chemotherapy action. Anticancer Res 1993 January; 13(1):103-6.

25. Kassouf W, Highshaw R, Nelkin GM, Dinney CP, Kamat AM. Vitamins C and K3 sensitize human urothelial tumors to gemcitabine. J Urol 2006 October;176(4 Pt 1):1642-7.

26. Tetef M, Margolin K, Ahn C, Akman S, Chow W, Coluzzi P, Leong L, Morgan RJ, Jr., Raschko J, Shibata S, . Mitomycin C and menadione for the treatment of advanced gastrointestinal cancers: a phase II trial. J Cancer Res Clin Oncol 1995;121(2):103-6.

27. Tetef M, Margolin K, Ahn C, Akman S, Chow W, Leong L, Morgan RJ, Jr., Raschko J, Somlo G, Doroshow JH. Mitomycin C and menadione for the treatment of lung cancer: a phase II trial. Invest New Drugs 1995;13(2):157-62.

28. Giunta R, Coppola A, Luongo C, Sammartino A, Guastafierro S, Grassia A, Giunta L, Mascolo L, Tirelli A, Coppola L. Ozonized autohemotransfusion improves hemorheological parameters and oxygen delivery to tissues in patients with peripheral occlusive arterial disease. Ann Hematol 2001 December;80(12):745-8.

29. Clavo B, Perez JL, Lopez L, Suarez G, Lloret M, Rodriguez V, Macias D, Santana M, Hernandez MA, Martin-Oliva R, Robaina F. Ozone Therapy for Tumor Oxygenation: a Pilot Study. Evid Based Complement Alternat Med 2004 June 1;1(1):93-8.

30. Bocci V, Larini A, Micheli V. Restoration of normoxia by ozone therapy may control neoplastic growth: a review and a working hypothesis. J Altern Complement Med 2005 April; 11(2):257-65.

31. Verdin-Vasquez RC, Zepeda-Perez C, Ferra-Ferrer R, Chavez-Negrete A, Contreras F, Barroso-Aranda J. Use of perftoran emulsion to decrease allogeneic blood transfusion in cardiac surgery: clinical trial. Artif Cells Blood Substit Immobil Biotechnol 2006;34(4):433-54.

32. Laurent A, Nicco C, Chereau C, Goulvestre C, Alexandre J, Alves A, Levy E, Goldwasser F, Panis Y, Soubrane O, Weill B, Batteux F. Controlling tumor growth by modulating endogenous production of reactive oxygen species. Cancer Res 2005 February 1;65(3):948-56.

33. Alexandre J, Batteux F, Nicco C, Chereau C, Laurent A, Guillevin L, Weill B, Goldwasser F. Accumulation of hydrogen peroxide is an early and crucial step for paclitaxel-induced cancer cell death both in vitro and in vivo. Int J Cancer 2006 July 1;119(1):41-8.

34. Ramanathan B, Jan KY, Chen CH, Hour TC, Yu HJ, Pu YS. Resistance to paclitaxel is proportional to cellular total antioxidant capacity. Cancer Res 2005 September; 15;65(18):8455-60.

35. Chan MM, Soprano KJ, Weinstein K, Fong D. Epigallocatechin-3-gallate delivers hydrogen peroxide to induce death of ovarian cancer cells and enhances their cisplatin susceptibility. J Cell Physiol 2006 May;207(2):389-96.

36. Teicher BA. Hypoxia and drug resistance. Cancer Metastasis Rev 1994 June;13(2):139-68.

37. Brown LM, Cowen RL, Debray C, Eustace A, Erler JT, Sheppard FC, Parker CA, Stratford IJ, Williams KJ. Reversing hypoxic cell chemoresistance in vitro using genetic and small molecule approaches targeting hypoxia inducible factor-1. Mol Pharmacol 2006 February; 69(2):411-8.

38. Erler JT, Cawthorne CJ, Williams KJ, Koritzinsky M, Wouters BG, Wilson C, Miller C, Demonacos C, Stratford IJ, Dive C. Hypoxia-mediated down-regulation of Bid and Bax in tumors occurs via hypoxia-inducible factor 1-dependent and -independent mechanisms and contributes to drug resistance. Mol Cell Biol 2004 April;24(7):2875-89.

39. Kopp E, Ghosh S. Inhibition of NF-kappa B by sodium salicylate and aspirin. Science 1994 August 12;265(5174):956-9.

40. Yin MJ, Yamamoto Y, Gaynor RB. The anti-inflammatory agents aspirin and salicylate inhibit the activity of I(kappa)B kinase-beta. Nature 1998 November 5;396(6706):77-80.

41. Aggarwal BB. Nuclear factor-kappaB: the enemy within. Cancer Cell 2004 September; 6(3):203-8.

42. Cusack JC, Liu R, Baldwin AS. NF- kappa B and chemoresistance: potentiation of cancer drugs via inhibition of NF- kappa B. Drug Resist Updat 1999 August;2(4):271-3.\

43. Whittle BJ, Hansen D, Salmon JA. Gastric ulcer formation and cyclo-oxygenase inhibition in cat antrum follows parenteral administration of aspirin but not salicylate. Eur J Pharmacol 1985 October 8;116(1-2):153-7.

44. Zambraski EJ, Atkinson DC, Diamond J. Effects of salicylate vs. aspirin on renal prostaglandins and function in normal and sodium-depleted dogs. J Pharmacol Exp Ther 1988 Oct;247(1):96-103.

45. Boettcher FA, Salvi RJ. Salicylate ototoxicity: review and synthesis. Am J Otolaryngol 1991 January;12(1):33-47.

46. McPherson TC. Salsalate for arthritis: a clinical evaluation. Clin Ther 1984;6(4):388-403.

47. Singh RP, Mallikarjuna GU, Sharma G, Dhanalakshmi S, Tyagi AK, Chan DC, Agarwal C, Agarwal R. Oral silibinin inhibits lung tumor growth in athymic nude mice and forms a novel chemocombination with doxorubicin targeting nuclear factor kappaB-mediated inducible chemoresistance. Clin Cancer Res 2004 December 15;10(24):8641-7.

48. Flaig TW, Su LJ, Harrison G, Agarwal R, Glode LM. Silibinin synergizes with mitoxantrone to inhibit cell growth and induce apoptosis in human prostate cancer cells. Int J Cancer 2007 May 1;120(9):2028-33.

49. Fakih M, Cao S, Durrani FA, Rustum YM. Selenium protects against toxicity induced by anticancer drugs and augments antitumor activity: a highly selective, new, and novel approach for the treatment of solid tumors. Clin Colorectal Cancer 2005 July;5(2):132-5.

50. Beer TM, Myrthue A. Calcitriol in cancer treatment: from the lab to the clinic. Mol Cancer Ther 2004 March;3(3):373-81.

51. Weitsman GE, Koren R, Zuck E, Rotem C, Liberman UA, Ravid A. Vitamin D sensitizes breast cancer cells to the action of H2O2: mitochondria as a convergence point in the death pathway. Free Radic Biol Med 2005 July 15;39(2):266-78.

52. Koren R, Hadari-Naor I, Zuck E, Rotem C, Liberman UA, Ravid A. Vitamin D is a prooxidant in breast cancer cells. Cancer Res 2001 February 15;61(4):1439-44.

Chapter Six – Modulating Cellular Signal Transduction

1. Alberts B, Johnson A, Lewis J, Raff M. Molecular Biology of the Cell. 4th ed. New York: Garland Science; 2002.

2. Suzuki YJ, Forman HJ, Sevanian A. Oxidants as stimulators of signal transduction. Free Radic Biol Med 1997;22(1-2):269-85.

3. Rhee SG, Bae YS, Lee SR, Kwon J. Hydrogen peroxide: a key messenger that modulates protein phosphorylation through cysteine oxidation. Sci STKE 2000 October 10;2000(53):E1.

4. Kim D, Dan HC, Park S, Yang L, Liu Q, Kaneko S, Ning J, He L, Yang H, Sun M, Nicosia SV, Cheng JQ. AKT/PKB signaling mechanisms in cancer and chemoresistance. Front Biosci 2005 January 1;10:975-87.

5. Jones PA, Baylin SB. The epigenomics of cancer. Cell 2007 February 23;128(4):683-92.

6. Press MF, Lenz HJ. EGFR, HER2 and VEGF pathways: validated targets for cancer treatment. Drugs 2007;67(14):2045-75.

7. Mellinghoff I. Why do cancer cells become "addicted" to oncogenic epidermal growth factor receptor? PLoS Med 2007 October;4(10):1620-2.

8. Paz K, Hadari YR. Targeted therapy of the insulin-like growth factor-1 receptor in cancer. Comb Chem High Throughput Screen 2008 January;11(1):62-9.

9. Vaquero EC, Edderkaoui M, Pandol SJ, Gukovsky I, Gukovskaya AS. Reactive oxygen species produced by NAD(P)H oxidase inhibit apoptosis in pancreatic cancer cells. J Biol Chem 2004 August 13;279(33):34643-54.

10. Wu WS. The signaling mechanism of ROS in tumor progression. Cancer Metastasis Rev 2006 December;25(4):695-705.

Chapter Seven – Oxidative Pre-conditioning Therapy: Ozone and UV Light

1. Leon OS, Menendez S, Merino N, Castillo R, Sam S, Perez L et al. Ozone oxidative preconditioning: a protection against cellular damage by free radicals. Mediators Inflamm 1998;7:289-94.

2. Bocci V, Valacchi G, Corradeschi F, Aldinucci C, Silvestri S, Paccagnini E et al. Studies on the biological effects of ozone: 7. Generation of reactive oxygen species (ROS) after exposure of human blood to ozone. J Biol Regul Homeost Agents 1998;12:67-75.

3. Borrego A, Zamora ZB, Gonzalez R, Romay C, Menendez S, Hernandez F et al. Protection by ozone preconditioning is mediated by the antioxidant system in cisplatin-induced nephrotoxicity in rats. Mediators Inflamm 2004;13:13-19.

4. Candelario-Jalil E, Mohammed-Al-Dalain S, Fernandez OS, Menendez S, Perez-Davison G, Merino N et al. Oxidative preconditioning affords protection against carbon tetrachloride-induced glycogen depletion and oxidative stress in rats. J Appl Toxicol 2001;21:297-301.

5. Al Dalain SM, Martinez G, Candelario-Jalil E, Menendez S, Re L, Giuliani A et al. Ozone treatment reduces markers of oxidative and endothelial damage in an experimental diabetes model in rats. Pharmacol Res 2001;44:391-96.

6. Ajamieh H, Merino N, Candelario-Jalil E, Menendez S, Martinez-Sanchez G, Re L et al. Similar protective effect of ischaemic and ozone oxidative preconditionings in liver ischaemia/reperfusion injury. Pharmacol Res 2002;45:333-39.

7. Ajamieh HH, Menendez S, Martinez-Sanchez G, Candelario-Jalil E, Re L, Giuliani A et al. Effects of ozone oxidative preconditioning on nitric oxide generation and cellular redox balance in a rat model of hepatic ischaemia-reperfusion. Liver Int 2004;24:55-62.

8. Zamora ZB, Borrego A, Lopez OY, Delgado R, Gonzalez R, Menendez S et al. Effects of ozone oxidative preconditioning on TNF-alpha release and antioxidant-prooxidant intracellular balance in mice during endotoxic shock. Mediators Inflamm 2005;2005:16-22.

Chapter Eight – IRT Anti-Inflammatory Therapies

1. Suh J, Rabson AB. NF-kappaB activation in human prostate cancer: important mediator or epiphenomenon? J Cell Biochem 2004;91:100-17.

2. Sclabas GM, Fujioka S, Schmidt C, Evans DB, Chiao PJ. NF-kappaB in pancreatic cancer. Int JGastrointest Cancer 2003;33:15-26.

3. Chang AA, Van Waes C. Nuclear factor-KappaB as a common target and activator of oncogenes in head and neck squamous cell carcinoma. Adv Otorhinolaryngol 2005;62:92-102.

4. Wu JT, Kral JG. The NF-kappaB/IkappaB signaling system: a molecular target in breast cancer therapy. J Surg Res 2005;123:158-69.

5. Yu YY, Li Q, Zhu ZG. NF-kappaB as a molecular target in adjuvant therapy of gastrointestinal carcinomas. Eur J Surg Oncol 2005;31:386-92.

6. Takada Y, Andreeff M, Aggarwal BB. Indole-3-carbinol suppresses NF-kappaB and IkappaBalpha kinase activation, causing inhibition of expression of NF-kappaB-regulated antiapoptotic and metastatic gene products and enhancement of apoptosis in myeloid and leukemia cells. Blood 2005;106:641-49.

7. Bentires-Alj M, Barbu V, Fillet M, Chariot A, Relic B, Jacobs N et al. NF-kappaB transcription factor induces drug resistance through MDR1 expression in cancer cells. Oncogene 2003;22:90-97.

8. Arlt A, Vorndamm J, Breitenbroich M, Folsch UR, Kalthoff H, Schmidt WE et al. Inhibition of NF-kappaB sensitizes human pancreatic carcinoma cells to apoptosis induced by etoposide (VP16) or doxorubicin. Oncogene 2001;20:859-68
.

9. Arlt A, Schafer H. NFkappaB-dependent chemoresistance in solid tumors. Int J Clin Pharmacol Ther 2002;40:336-47.

10. Jung M, Dritschilo A. NF-kappa B signaling pathway as a target for human tumor radiosensitization. Semin Radiat Oncol 2001;11:346-51.

11. Nakanishi C, Toi M. Nuclear factor-kappaB inhibitors as sensitizers to anticancer drugs. Nat Rev Cancer 2005;5:297-309.

12. Huang S, Robinson JB, Deguzman A, Bucana CD, Fidler IJ. Blockade of nuclear factor-kappaB signaling inhibits angiogenesis and tumorigenicity of human ovarian cancer cells by suppressing expression of vascular endothelial growth factor and interleukin 8. Cancer Res 2000;60:5334-39.

13. Duque J, Diaz-Munoz MD, Fresno M, Iniguez MA. Up-regulation of cyclooxygenase-2 by interleukin-1beta in colon carcinoma cells. Cell Signal 2006;18:1262-69.

14. Chell S, Kadi A, Williams AC, Paraskeva C. Mediators of PGE2 synthesis and signalling downstream of COX-2 represent potential targets for the prevention/treatment of colorectal cancer. Biochim.Biophys Acta 2006;1766:104-19.

15. Sminia P, Kuipers G, Geldof A, Lafleur V, Slotman B. COX-2 inhibitors act as radiosensitizer in tumor treatment. Biomed Pharmacother 2005;59 Suppl 2:S272-S275.

16. Meric JB, Rottey S, Olaussen K, Soria JC, Khayat D, Rixe O et al. Cyclooxygenase-2 as a target for anticancer drug development. Crit Rev Oncol Hematol 2006;59:51-64.

17. Nie D. Cyclooxygenases and lipoxygenases in prostate and breast cancers. Front Biosci 2007;12:1574-85.

18. Eisinger AL, Prescott SM, Jones DA, Stafforini DM. The role of cyclooxygenase-2 and prostaglandins in colon cancer. Prostaglandins Other Lipid Mediat 2007;82:147-54.

19. Liao Z, Mason KA, Milas L. Cyclo-oxygenase-2 and its inhibition in cancer : is there a role? Drugs 2007;67:821-45.

20. Zeddou M, Greimers R, de Valensart N, Nayjib B, Tasken K, Boniver J et al. Prostaglandin E2 induces the expression of functional inhibitory CD94/NKG2A receptors in human CD8+ T lymphocytes by a cAMP-dependent protein kinase A type I pathway. Biochem Pharmacol 2005;70:714-24.

21. Klein S, de Fougerolles AR, Blaikie P, Khan L, Pepe A, Green CD et al. Alpha 5 beta 1 integrin activates an NF-kappa B-dependent program of gene expression important for angiogenesis and inflammation. Mol Cell Biol 2002;22:5912-22.

22. Gately S, Li WW. Multiple roles of COX-2 in tumor angiogenesis: a target for antiangiogenic therapy. Semin Oncol 2004;31:2-11.

23. Williams CS, Tsujii M, Reese J, Dey SK, DuBois RN. Host cyclooxygenase-2 modulates carcinoma growth. J Clin Invest 2000;105:1589-94.

24. Tisdale MJ. Cancer cachexia. Langenbecks Arch Surg 2004;389:299-305.

25. Whittle BJ, Hansen D, Salmon JA. Gastric ulcer formation and cyclo-oxygenase inhibition in cat antrum follows parenteral administration of aspirin but not salicylate. Eur J Pharmacol 1985;116:153-57.

26. Zambraski EJ, Atkinson DC, Diamond J. Effects of salicylate vs. aspirin on renal prostaglandins and function in normal and sodium-depleted dogs. J Pharmacol Exp Ther 1988;247:96-103.

27. Cryer B, Goldschmiedt M, Redfern JS, Feldman M. Comparison of salsalate and aspirin on mucosal injury and gastroduodenal mucosal prostaglandins. Gastroenterology 1990;99:1616-21.

28. Kopp E, Ghosh S. Inhibition of NF-kappa B by sodium salicylate and aspirin. Science 1994;265:956-59.

29. Yin MJ, Yamamoto Y, Gaynor RB. The anti-inflammatory agents aspirin and salicylate inhibit the activity of I(kappa)B kinase-beta. Nature 1998;396:77-80.

30. Borthwick GM, Johnson AS, Partington M, Burn J, Wilson R, Arthur HM. Therapeutic levels of aspirin and salicylate directly inhibit a model of angiogenesis through a Cox-independent mechanism. FASEB J 2006;20:2009-16.

31. McCarty MF, Block KI. Preadministration of high-dose salicylates, suppressors of NF-kappaB activation, may increase the chemosensitivity of many cancers: an example of proapoptotic signal modulation therapy. Integr.Cancer Ther 2006;5:252-68.

32. McCarty MF, Block KI. Toward a core nutraceutical program for cancer management. Integr.Cancer Ther 2006;5:150-71.

33. McPherson TC. Salsalate for arthritis: a clinical evaluation. Clin Ther 1984;6:388-403.

34. Boettcher FA, Salvi RJ. Salicylate ototoxicity: review and synthesis. Am J Otolaryngol 1991;12:33-47.

35. Lovborg H, Oberg F, Rickardson L, Gullbo J, Nygren P, Larsson R. Inhibition of proteasome activity, nuclear factor-KappaB translocation and cell survival by the antialcoholism drug disulfiram. Int J Cancer 2006;118:1577-80.

36. Chen D, Cui QC, Yang H, Dou QP. Disulfiram, a clinically used anti-alcoholism drug and copper-binding agent, induces apoptotic cell death in breast cancer cultures and xenografts via inhibition of the proteasome activity. Cancer Res 2006;66:10425-33.

37. Zavrski I, Kleeberg L, Kaiser M, Fleissner C, Heider U, Sterz J et al. Proteasome as an emerging therapeutic target in cancer. Curr Pharm Des 2007;13:471-85.

38. Cryer B, Feldman M. Cyclooxygenase-1 and cyclooxygenase-2 selectivity of widely used nonsteroidal anti-inflammatory drugs. Am J Med 1998;104:413-21.

39. Van Hecken A, Schwartz JI, Depre M, de L, I, Dallob A, Tanaka W et al. Comparative inhibitory activity of rofecoxib, meloxicam, diclofenac, ibuprofen, and naproxen on COX-2 versus COX-1 in healthy volunteers. J Clin Pharmacol 2000;40:1109-20.

40. Jick SS, Kaye JA, Jick H. Diclofenac and acute myocardial infarction in patients with no major risk factors. Br J Clin Pharmacol 2007; Nov;64(5):662-7.

Chapter Nine – Metronomic Therapy

1. Browder T, Butterfield CE, Kraling BM, Shi B, Marshall B, O'Reilly MS et al. Antiangiogenic scheduling of chemotherapy improves efficacy against experimental drug-resistant cancer. Cancer Res 2000;60:1878-86.

2. Klement G, Baruchel S, Rak J, Man S, Clark K, Hicklin DJ et al. Continuous low-dose therapy with vinblastine and VEGF receptor-2 antibody induces sustained tumor regression without overt toxicity. J Clin Invest 2000;105:R15-R24.

3. Ghiringhelli F, Menard C, Puig PE, Ladoire S, Roux S, Martin F et al. Metronomic cyclophosphamide regimen selectively depletes CD4+CD25+ regulatory T cells and restores T and NK effector functions in end stage cancer patients. Cancer Immunol Immunother 2007;56:641-48.

4. Beyer M, Schultze JL. Regulatory T cells in cancer. Blood 2006;108:804-11.

5. Ghiringhelli F, Menard C, Martin F, Zitvogel L. The role of regulatory T cells in the control of natural killer cells: relevance during tumor progression. Immunol Rev 2006;214:229-38.

6. Kerbel RS, Kamen BA. The anti-angiogenic basis of metronomic chemotherapy. Nat Rev Cancer 2004;4:423-36.

7. Gille J, Spieth K, Kaufmann R. Metronomic low-dose chemotherapy as antiangiogenic therapeutic strategy for cancer. J Dtsch Dermatol Ges 2005;3:26-32.

8. Pietras K, Hanahan D. A multitargeted, metronomic, and maximum-tolerated dose "chemo-switch" regimen is antiangiogenic, producing objective responses and survival benefit in a mouse model of cancer. J Clin Oncol 2005;23:939-52.

9. Shaked Y, Emmenegger U, Francia G, Chen L, Lee CR, Man S et al. Low-dose metronomic combined with intermittent bolus-dose cyclophosphamide is an effective long-term chemotherapy treatment strategy. Cancer Res 2005;65:7045-51.

10. Colleoni M, Rocca A, Sandri MT, Zorzino L, Masci G, Nole F et al. Low-dose oral methotrexate and cyclophosphamide in metastatic breast cancer: antitumor activity and correlation with vascular endothelial growth factor levels. Ann Oncol 2002;13:73-80.

11. Orlando L, Cardillo A, Rocca A, Balduzzi A, Ghisini R, Peruzzotti G et al. Prolonged clinical benefit with metronomic chemotherapy in patients with metastatic breast cancer. Anticancer Drugs 2006;17:961-67.

Chapter Ten – IRT Nutraceuticals for Cancer Control

1. Maestroni GJ. The immunotherapeutic potential of melatonin. Expert Opin Investig Drugs 2001;10:467-76.

2. Miller SC, Pandi-Perumal SR, Esquifino AI, Cardinali DP, Maestroni GJ. The role of melatonin in immuno-enhancement: potential application in cancer. Int J Exp Pathol 2006;87:81-87.

3. Wu J, Lanier LL. Natural killer cells and cancer. Adv Cancer Res 2003;90:127-56.

4. Hallett WH, Murphy WJ. Natural killer cells: biology and clinical use in cancer therapy. Cell Mol Immunol 2004;1:12-21.

5. Maestroni GJ, Conti A, Pierpaoli W. Pineal melatonin, its fundamental immunoregulatory role in aging and cancer. Ann NY Acad Sci 1988;521:140-48.

6. Rodriguez C, Mayo JC, Sainz RM, Antolin I, Herrera F, Martin V et al. Regulation of antioxidant enzymes: a significant role for melatonin. J Pineal Res 2004;36:1-9.

7. Hardeland R. Antioxidative protection by melatonin: multiplicity of mechanisms from radical detoxification to radical avoidance. Endocrine 2005;27:119-30.

8. Oz E, Ilhan MN. Effects of melatonin in reducing the toxic effects of doxorubicin. Mol Cell Biochem 2006;286:11-15.

9. Kim C, Kim N, Joo H, Youm JB, Park WS, Cuong DV et al. Modulation by melatonin of the cardiotoxic and antitumor activities of adriamycin. J Cardiovasc Pharmacol 2005;46:200-10.

10. Atessahin A, Sahna E, Turk G, Ceribasi AO, Yilmaz S, Yuce A et al. Chemoprotective effect of melatonin against cisplatin-induced testicular toxicity in rats. J Pineal Res 2006;41:21-27.

11. Hara M, Yoshida M, Nishijima H, Yokosuka M, Iigo M, Ohtani-Kaneko R et al. Melatonin, a pineal secretory product with antioxidant properties, protects against cisplatin-induced nephrotoxicity in rats. J Pineal Res 2001;30:129-38.

12. Lissoni P, Paolorossi F, Ardizzoia A, Barni S, Chilelli M, Mancuso M et al. A randomized study of chemotherapy with cisplatin plus etoposide versus chemoendocrine therapy with cisplatin, etoposide and the pineal hormone melatonin as a first-line treatment of advanced non-small cell lung cancer patients in a poor clinical state. J Pineal Res 1997;23:15-19.

13. Anwar MM, Mahfouz HA, Sayed AS. Potential protective effects of melatonin on bone marrow of rats exposed to cytotoxic drugs. Comp Biochem Physiol A Mol Integr Physiol 1998;119:493-501.

14. Lissoni P, Barni S, Ardizzoia A, Tancini G, Conti A, Maestroni G. A randomized study with the pineal hormone melatonin versus supportive care alone in patients with brain metastases due to solid neoplasms. Cancer 1994;73:699-701.

15. Lissoni P, Meregalli S, Nosetto L, Barni S, Tancini G, Fossati V et al. Increased survival time in brain glioblastomas by a radioneuroendocrine strategy with radiotherapy plus melatonin compared to radiotherapy alone. Oncology 1996;53:43-46.

16. Cerea G, Vaghi M, Ardizzoia A, Villa S, Bucovec R, Mengo S et al. Biomodulation of cancer chemotherapy for metastatic colorectal cancer: a randomized study of weekly low-dose irinotecan alone versus irinotecan plus the oncostatic pineal hormone melatonin in metastatic colorectal cancer patients progressing on 5-fluorouracil-containing combinations. Anticancer Res 2003;23:1951-54.

17. Lissoni P, Chilelli M, Villa S, Cerizza L, Tancini G. Five years survival in metastatic non-small cell lung cancer patients treated with chemotherapy alone or chemotherapy and melatonin: a randomized trial. J Pineal Res 2003;35:12-15.

18. Lissoni P. Biochemotherapy with standard chemotherapies plus the pineal hormone melatonin in the treatment of advanced solid neoplasms. Pathol Biol (Paris). 2007; Apr-May;55(3-4):201-4.

19. Lissoni P, Paolorossi F, Tancini G, Barni S, Ardizzoia A, Brivio F et al. Is there a role for melatonin in the treatment of neoplastic cachexia? Eur J Cancer 1996;32A:1340-43.

20. Simopoulos AP. Omega-3 fatty acids in inflammation and autoimmune diseases. J Am Coll Nutr 2002;21:495-505.

21. Zeller FP, Spears C. Fish oil: effectiveness as a dietary supplement in the prevention of heart disease. Drug Intell Clin Pharm 1987;21:584-89.

22. Rose DP, Connolly JM, Liu XH. Fatty acid regulation of breast cancer cell growth and invasion. Adv Exp Med Biol 1997;422:47-55.

23. Hardman WE. (n-3) fatty acids and cancer therapy. J Nutr 2004;134:3427S-30S.

24. Wen B, Deutsch E, Opolon P, Auperin A, Frascogna V, Connault E et al. n-3 polyunsaturated fatty acids decrease mucosal/epidermal reactions and enhance antitumour effect of ionising radiation with inhibition of tumour angiogenesis. Br J Cancer 2003;89:1102-07.

25. Hardman WE, Sun L, Short N, Cameron IL. Dietary omega-3 fatty acids and ionizing irradiation on human breast cancer xenograft growth and angiogenesis. Cancer Cell Int 2005;5:12.

26. McCarty MF. Fish oil may impede tumour angiogenesis and invasiveness by down-regulating protein kinase C and modulating eicosanoid production. Med Hypotheses 1996;46:107-15.

27. Rose DP, Connolly JM. Regulation of tumor angiogenesis by dietary fatty acids and eicosanoids. Nutr Cancer 2000;37:119-27.

28. Murota SI, Onodera M, Morita I. Regulation of angiogenesis by controlling VEGF receptor. Ann NY Acad Sci 2000;902:208-12.

29. Shtivelband MI, Juneja HS, Lee S, Wu KK. Aspirin and salicylate inhibit colon cancer medium- and VEGF-induced endothelial tube formation: correlation with suppression of cyclooxygenase-2 expression. J Thromb Haemost 2003;1:2225-33.

30. Liao Z, Mason KA, Milas L. Cyclo-oxygenase-2 and its inhibition in cancer : is there a role? Drugs 2007;67:821-45.

31. Claria J, Romano M. Pharmacological intervention of cyclooxygenase-2 and 5-lipoxygenase pathways. Impact on inflammation and cancer. Curr Pharm Des 2005;11:3431-47.

32. Tisdale MJ. Inhibition of lipolysis and muscle protein degradation by EPA in cancer cachexia. Nutrition 1996;12:S31-S33.

33. Whitehouse AS, Smith HJ, Drake JL, Tisdale MJ. Mechanism of attenuation of skeletal muscle protein catabolism in cancer cachexia by eicosapentaenoic acid. Cancer Res 2001;61:3604-09.

34. Wigmore SJ, Barber MD, Ross JA, Tisdale MJ, Fearon KC. Effect of oral eicosapentaenoic acid on weight loss in patients with pancreatic cancer. Nutr Cancer 2000;36:177-84.

35. Fearon KC, von Meyenfeldt MF, Moses AG, Van Geenen R, Roy A, Gouma DJ et al. Effect of a protein and energy dense N-3 fatty acid enriched oral supplement on loss of weight and lean tissue in cancer cachexia: a randomised double blind trial. Gut 2003;52:1479-86.

36. Pardini RS. Nutritional intervention with omega-3 fatty acids enhances tumor response to anti-neoplastic agents. Chem Biol Interact 2006;162:89-105.

37. Colas S, Paon L, Denis F, Prat M, Louisot P, Hoinard C et al. Enhanced radiosensitivity of rat autochthonous mammary tumors by dietary docosahexaenoic acid. Int J Cancer 2004;109:449-54.

38. Townsend K, Banwell CM, Guy M, Colston KW, Mansi JL, Stewart PM et al. Autocrine metabolism of vitamin D in normal and malignant breast tissue. Clin Cancer Res 2005;11:3579-86.

39. Townsend K, Evans KN, Campbell MJ, Colston KW, Adams JS, Hewison M. Biological actions of extra-renal 25-hydroxyvitamin D-1alpha-hydroxylase and implications for chemoprevention and treatment. J Steroid Biochem Mol Biol 2005;97:103-09.

40. Banerjee P, Chatterjee M. Antiproliferative role of vitamin D and its analogs--a brief overview. Mol Cell Biochem 2003;253:247-54.

41. Holick MF. Environmental factors that influence the cutaneous production of vitamin D. Am J Clin Nutr JID - 0376027 1995;61:638S-45S.

42. Vieth R. Vitamin D supplementation, 25-hydroxyvitamin D concentrations, and safety. Am J Clin Nutr JID - 0376027 1999;69:842-56.

43. Holick MF. Vitamin D: importance in the prevention of cancers, type 1 diabetes, heart disease, and osteoporosis. Am J Clin Nutr 2004;79:362-71.

44. Giovannucci E. The epidemiology of vitamin D and cancer incidence and mortality: a review (United States). Cancer Causes Control 2005;16:83-95.

45. Garland CF, Garland FC, Gorham ED, Lipkin M, Newmark H, Mohr SB et al. The role of vitamin D in cancer prevention. Am J Public Health 2006;96:252-61.

46. Krause R, Matulla-Nolte B, Essers M, Brown A, Hopfenmuller W. UV radiation and cancer prevention: what is the evidence? Anticancer Res 2006;26:2723-27.

47. Schwartz GG, Skinner HG. Vitamin D status and cancer: new insights. Curr.Opin. Clin Nutr Metab Care 2007;10:6-11.

48. Grant WB, Garland CF, Gorham ED. An estimate of cancer mortality rate reductions in Europe and the US with 1,000 IU of oral vitamin D per day. Recent Results Cancer Res 2007;174:225-34.

49. Grant WB. An estimate of premature cancer mortality in the U.S. due to inadequate doses of solar ultraviolet-B radiation. Cancer 2002;94:1867-75.

50. Friedrich M, Rafi L, Mitschele T, Tilgen W, Schmidt W, Reichrath J. Analysis of the vitamin D system in cervical carcinomas, breast cancer and ovarian cancer. Recent Results Cancer Res 2003;164:239-46.

51. Diaz GD, Paraskeva C, Thomas MG, Binderup L, Hague A. Apoptosis is induced by the active metabolite of vitamin D3 and its analogue EB1089 in colorectal adenoma and carcinoma cells: possible implications for prevention and therapy. Cancer Res 2000;60:2304-12.

52. Guzey M, Kitada S, Reed JC. Apoptosis induction by 1alpha,25-dihydroxyvitamin D3 in prostate cancer. Mol Cancer Ther 2002;1:667-77.

53. Wagner N, Wagner KD, Schley G, Badiali L, Theres H, Scholz H. 1,25-dihydroxyvitamin D3-induced apoptosis of retinoblastoma cells is associated with reciprocal changes of Bcl-2 and bax. Exp Eye Res 2003;77:1-9.

54. Wang Q, Yang W, Uytingco MS, Christakos S, Wieder R. 1,25-Dihydroxyvitamin D3 and all-trans-retinoic acid sensitize breast cancer cells to chemotherapy-induced cell death. Cancer Res 2000;60:2040-48.

55. Hershberger PA, Yu WD, Modzelewski RA, Rueger RM, Johnson CS, Trump DL. Calcitriol (1,25-dihydroxycholecalciferol) enhances paclitaxel antitumor activity in vitro and in vivo and accelerates paclitaxel-induced apoptosis. Clin Cancer Res 2001;7:1043-51.

56. Dunlap N, Schwartz GG, Eads D, Cramer SD, Sherk AB, John V et al. 1alpha,25-dihydroxyvitamin D(3) (calcitriol) and its analogue, 19-nor-1alpha,25(OH)(2)D(2), potentiate the effects of ionising radiation on human prostate cancer cells. Br J Cancer 2003;89:746-53.

57. DeMasters GA, Gupta MS, Jones KR, Cabot M, Wang H, Gennings C et al. Potentiation of cell killing by fractionated radiation and suppression of proliferative recovery in MCF-7 breast tumor cells by the Vitamin D3 analog EB 1089. J Steroid Biochem Mol Biol 2004;92:365-74.

58. Lim HS, Roychoudhuri R, Peto J, Schwartz G, Baade P, Moller H. Cancer survival is dependent on season of diagnosis and sunlight exposure. Int J Cancer 2006;119:1530-36.

59. Porojnicu A, Robsahm TE, Berg JP, Moan J. Season of diagnosis is a predictor of cancer survival. Sun-induced vitamin D may be involved: a possible role of sun-induced Vitamin D. J Steroid Biochem Mol Biol 2007;103:675-78.

60. Zhou W, Heist RS, Liu G, Asomaning K, Neuberg DS, Hollis BW et al. Circulating 25-hydroxyvitamin D levels predict survival in early-stage non-small-cell lung cancer patients. J Clin Oncol 2007;25:479-85.

61. Woo TC, Choo R, Jamieson M, Chander S, Vieth R. Pilot study: potential role of vitamin D (Cholecalciferol) in patients with PSA relapse after definitive therapy. Nutr Cancer 2005;51:32-36.

62. Zi X, Zhang J, Agarwal R, Pollak M. Silibinin up-regulates insulin-like growth factor-binding protein 3 expression and inhibits proliferation of androgen-independent prostate cancer cells. Cancer Res 2000;60:5617-20.

63. Kang SN, Lee MH, Kim KM, Cho D, Kim TS. Induction of human promyelocytic leukemia HL-60 cell differentiation into monocytes by silibinin: involvement of protein kinase C. Biochem Pharmacol 2001;61:1487-95.

64. Sharma G, Singh RP, Chan DC, Agarwal R. Silibinin induces growth inhibition and apoptotic cell death in human lung carcinoma cells. Anticancer Res 2003;23:2649-55.

65. Qi L, Singh RP, Lu Y, Agarwal R, Harrison GS, Franzusoff A et al. Epidermal growth factor receptor mediates silibinin-induced cytotoxicity in a rat glioma cell line. Cancer Biol Ther 2003;2:526-31.

66. Agarwal C, Singh RP, Dhanalakshmi S, Tyagi AK, Tecklenburg M, Sclafani RA et al. Silibinin upregulates the expression of cyclin-dependent kinase inhibitors and causes cell cycle arrest and apoptosis in human colon carcinoma HT-29 cells. Oncogene 2003;22:8271-82.

67. Tyagi AK, Agarwal C, Singh RP, Shroyer KR, Glode LM, Agarwal R. Silibinin down-regulates survivin protein and mRNA expression and causes caspases activation and apoptosis in human bladder transitional-cell papilloma RT4 cells. Biochem Biophys Res Commun 2003;312:1178-84.

68. Varghese L, Agarwal C, Tyagi A, Singh RP, Agarwal R. Silibinin efficacy against human hepatocellular carcinoma. Clin Cancer Res 2005;11:8441-48.

69. Lee SO, Jeong YJ, Im HG, Kim CH, Chang YC, Lee IS. Silibinin suppresses PMA-induced MMP-9 expression by blocking the AP-1 activation via MAPK signaling pathways in MCF-7 human breast carcinoma cells. Biochem.Biophys.Res.Commun 2007;354:165-71.

70. Tyagi AK, Agarwal C, Chan DC, Agarwal R. Synergistic anti-cancer effects of silibinin with conventional cytotoxic agents doxorubicin, cisplatin and carboplatin against human breast carcinoma MCF-7 and MDA-MB468 cells. Oncol Rep 2004;11:493-99.

71. Singh RP, Agarwal R. A cancer chemopreventive agent silibinin, targets mitogenic and survival signaling in prostate cancer. Mutat Res 2004;555:21-32.

72. Hannay JA, Yu D. Silibinin: a thorny therapeutic for EGF-R expressing tumors? Cancer Biol Ther 2003;2:532-33.

73. Singh RP, Dhanalakshmi S, Tyagi AK, Chan DC, Agarwal C, Agarwal R. Dietary feeding of silibinin inhibits advance human prostate carcinoma growth in athymic nude mice and increases plasma insulin-like growth factor-binding protein-3 levels. Cancer Res 2002;62:3063-69.

74. Singh RP, Dhanalakshmi S, Agarwal C, Agarwal R. Silibinin strongly inhibits growth and survival of human endothelial cells via cell cycle arrest and downregulation of survivin, Akt and NF-kappaB: implications for angioprevention and antiangiogenic therapy. Oncogene 2005;24:1188-202.

75. Polyak SJ, Morishima C, Shuhart MC, Wang CC, Liu Y, Lee DY. Inhibition of T-cell inflammatory cytokines, hepatocyte NF-kappaB signaling, and HCV infection by standardized silymarin. Gastroenterology 2007;132:1925-36.

76. Aggarwal BB. Nuclear factor-kappaB: the enemy within. Cancer Cell 2004;6:203-08.

77. Arlt A, Schafer H. NFkappaB-dependent chemoresistance in solid tumors. Int.J Clin Pharmacol Ther 2002;40:336-47.

78. Singh RP, Sharma G, Dhanalakshmi S, Agarwal C, Agarwal R. Suppression of advanced human prostate tumor growth in athymic mice by silibinin feeding is associated with reduced cell proliferation, increased apoptosis, and inhibition of angiogenesis. Cancer Epidemiol Biomarkers Prev 2003;12:933-39.

79. Gallo D, Giacomelli S, Ferlini C, Raspaglio G, Apollonio P, Prislei S et al. Antitumour activity of the silybin-phosphatidylcholine complex, IdB 1016, against human ovarian cancer. Eur J Cancer 2003;39:2403-10.

80. Yang SH, Lin JK, Chen WS, Chiu JH. Anti-angiogenic effect of silymarin on colon cancer LoVo cell line. J Surg Res 2003;113:133-38.

82. Combs GF, Jr., Gray WP. Chemopreventive agents: selenium. Pharmacol Ther 1998;79:179-92.

83. Clark LC, Combs GF, Jr., Turnbull BW, Slate EH, Chalker DK, Chow J et al. Effects of selenium supplementation for cancer prevention in patients with carcinoma of the skin. A randomized controlled trial. Nutritional Prevention of Cancer Study Group. JAMA 1996;276:1957-63.

84. Clark LC. The epidemiology of selenium and cancer. Fed Proc 1985;44:2584-89.

85. Etminan M, FitzGerald JM, Gleave M, Chambers K. Intake of selenium in the prevention of prostate cancer: a systematic review and meta-analysis. Cancer Causes Control 2005;16:1125-31.

86. Stadtman TC. Selenium biochemistry. Mammalian selenoenzymes. Ann NY Acad Sci 2000;899:399-402.

87. Fakih M, Cao S, Durrani FA, Rustum YM. Selenium protects against toxicity induced by anticancer drugs and augments antitumor activity: a highly selective, new, and novel approach for the treatment of solid tumors. Clin Colorectal Cancer 2005;5:132-35.

88. Shin SH, Yoon MJ, Kim M, Kim JI, Lee SJ, Lee YS et al. Enhanced lung cancer cell killing by the combination of selenium and ionizing radiation. Oncol Rep 2007;17:209-16.

89. Fischer JL, Mihelc EM, Pollok KE, Smith ML. Chemotherapeutic selectivity conferred by selenium: a role for p53-dependent DNA repair. Mol Cancer Ther 2007;6:355-61.

90. Kiremidjian-Schumacher L, Roy M, Wishe HI, Cohen MW, Stotzky G. Supplementation with selenium and human immune cell functions. II. Effect on cytotoxic lymphocytes and natural killer cells. Biol Trace Elem Res 1994;41:115-27.

91. Kiremidjian-Schumacher L, Roy M, Wishe HI, Cohen MW, Stotzky G. Supplementation with selenium augments the functions of natural killer and lymphokine-activated killer cells. Biol. Trace Elem Res 1996;52:227-39.

92. Cao Y, Cao R. Angiogenesis inhibited by drinking tea. Nature 1999;398:381.

93. Jung YD, Kim MS, Shin BA, Chay KO, Ahn BW, Liu W et al. EGCG, a major component of green tea, inhibits tumour growth by inhibiting VEGF induction in human colon carcinoma cells. Br J Cancer 2001;84:844-50.

94. Jung YD, Ellis LM. Inhibition of tumour invasion and angiogenesis by epigallocatechin gallate (EGCG), a major component of green tea. Int J Exp Pathol 2001;82:309-16.

95. Pisters KM, Newman RA, Coldman B, Shin DM, Khuri FR, Hong WK et al. Phase I trial of oral green tea extract in adult patients with solid tumors. J Clin Oncol 2001;19:1830-38.

96. Lamy S, Gingras D, Beliveau R. Green tea catechins inhibit vascular endothelial growth factor receptor phosphorylation. Cancer Res 2002;62:381-85.

97. Aggarwal BB, Kumar A, Bharti AC. Anticancer potential of curcumin: preclinical and clinical studies. Anticancer Res 2003;23:363-98.

98. Singh S, Khar A. Biological effects of curcumin and its role in cancer chemoprevention and therapy. Anticancer Agents Med Chem 2006;6:259-70.

Integrative Regulatory Therapy

99. LoTempio MM, Veena MS, Steele HL, Ramamurthy B, Ramalingam TS, Cohen AN et al. Curcumin suppresses growth of head and neck squamous cell carcinoma. Clin Cancer Res 2005;11:6994-7002.

100. Hong JH, Ahn KS, Bae E, Jeon SS, Choi HY. The effects of curcumin on the invasiveness of prostate cancer in vitro and in vivo. Prostate Cancer Prostatic Dis 2006;9:147-52.

101. Li L, Ahmed B, Mehta K, Kurzrock R. Liposomal curcumin with and without oxaliplatin: effects on cell growth, apoptosis, and angiogenesis in colorectal cancer. Mol Cancer Ther 2007;6:1276-82.

102. Kawamori T, Lubet R, Steele VE, Kelloff GJ, Kaskey RB, Rao CV et al. Chemopreventive effect of curcumin, a naturally occurring anti-inflammatory agent, during the promotion/progression stages of colon cancer. Cancer Res 1999;59:597-601.

103. Bhardwaj RK, Glaeser H, Becquemont L, Klotz U, Gupta SK, Fromm MF. Piperine, a major constituent of black pepper, inhibits human P-glycoprotein and CYP3A4. J Pharmacol Exp Ther 2002;302:645-50.

104. Shoba G, Joy D, Joseph T, Majeed M, Rajendran R, Srinivas PS. Influence of piperine on the pharmacokinetics of curcumin in animals and human volunteers. Planta Med 1998;64:353-56.

105. Lambert JD, Hong J, Kim DH, Mishin VM, Yang CS. Piperine enhances the bioavailability of the tea polyphenol (-)-epigallocatechin-3-gallate in mice. J Nutr 2004;134:1948-52.

106. Singh RP, Tyagi AK, Dhanalakshmi S, Agarwal R, Agarwal C. Grape seed extract inhibits advanced human prostate tumor growth and angiogenesis and upregulates insulin-like growth factor binding protein-3. Int J Cancer 2004;108:733-40.

107. Kaur M, Singh RP, Gu M, Agarwal R, Agarwal C. Grape seed extract inhibits in vitro and in vivo growth of human colorectal carcinoma cells. Clin Cancer Res 2006;12:6194-202.

108. Manna SK, Mukhopadhyay A, Aggarwal BB. Resveratrol suppresses TNF-induced activation of nuclear transcription factors NF-kappa B, activator protein-1, and apoptosis: potential role of reactive oxygen intermediates and lipid peroxidation. J Immunol 2000;164:6509-19.

109. Bogden JD. Influence of zinc on immunity in the elderly. J Nutr Health Aging 2004;8:48-54.

110. Ammon HP. Boswellic acids in chronic inflammatory diseases. Planta Med 2006;72:1100-16.

111. Safayhi H, Sailer ER, Ammon HP. Mechanism of 5-lipoxygenase inhibition by acetyl-11-keto-beta-boswellic acid. Mol Pharmacol 1995;47:1212-16.

112. Ghosh J, Myers CE. Inhibition of arachidonate 5-lipoxygenase triggers massive apoptosis in human prostate cancer cells. Proc Natl Acad Sci USA 1998;95:13182-87.

113. Ding XZ, Tong WG, Adrian TE. Multiple signal pathways are involved in the mitogenic effect of 5(S)-HETE in human pancreatic cancer. Oncology 2003;65:285-94.

114. Ihara A, Wada K, Yoneda M, Fujisawa N, Takahashi H, Nakajima A. Blockade of leukotriene B4 signaling pathway induces apoptosis and suppresses cell proliferation in colon cancer. J Pharmacol Sci 2007;103:24-32.

115. Tong WG, Ding XZ, Witt RC, Adrian TE. Lipoxygenase inhibitors attenuate growth of human pancreatic cancer xenografts and induce apoptosis through the mitochondrial pathway. Mol Cancer Ther 2002;1:929-35.

116. Tsukada T, Nakashima K, Shirakawa S. Arachidonate 5-lipoxygenase inhibitors show potent antiproliferative effects on human leukemia cell lines. Biochem. Biophys Res Commun 1986;140:832-36.

117. Ghosh J, Myers CE. Arachidonic acid stimulates prostate cancer cell growth: critical role of 5-lipoxygenase. Biochem.Biophys.Res Commun 1997;235:418-23.

118. Avis I, Hong SH, Martinez A, Moody T, Choi YH, Trepel J et al. Five-lipoxygenase inhibitors can mediate apoptosis in human breast cancer cell lines through complex eicosanoid interactions. FASEB J 2001;15:2007-09.

119. Fan XM, Tu SP, Lam SK, Wang WP, Wu J, Wong WM et al. Five-lipoxygenase-activating protein inhibitor MK-886 induces apoptosis in gastric cancer through upregulation of p27kip1 and bax. J Gastroenterol Hepatol 2004;19:31-37.

120. Hoque A, Lippman SM, Wu TT, Xu Y, Liang ZD, Swisher S et al Increased 5-lipoxygenase expression and induction of apoptosis by its inhibitors in esophageal cancer: a potential target for prevention. Carcinogenesis 2005;26:785-91.

121. Matsuyama M, Yoshimura R, Mitsuhashi M, Tsuchida K, Takemoto Y, Kawahito Y et al. 5-Lipoxygenase inhibitors attenuate growth of human renal cell carcinoma and induce apoptosis through arachidonic acid pathway. Oncol Rep 2005;14:73-79.

122. Hayashi T, Nishiyama K, Shirahama T. Inhibition of 5-lipoxygenase pathway suppresses the growth of bladder cancer cells. Int J Urol 2006;13:1086-91.

123. Catalano A, Caprari P, Soddu S, Procopio A, Romano M. 5-lipoxygenase antagonizes genotoxic stress-induced apoptosis by altering p53 nuclear trafficking. FASEB J 2004;18:1740-42.

124. Wenger FA, Kilian M, Bisevac M, Khodadayan C, von Seebach M, Schimke I et al. Effects of Celebrex and Zyflo on liver metastasis and lipidperoxidation in pancreatic cancer in Syrian hamsters. Clin Exp Metastasis 2002;19:681-87.

125. Liu JJ, Nilsson A, Oredsson S, Badmaev V, Zhao WZ, Duan RD. Boswellic acids trigger apoptosis via a pathway dependent on caspase-8 activation but independent on Fas/Fas ligand interaction in colon cancer HT-29 cells. Carcinogenesi. 2002;23:2087-93.

126. Zhao W, Entschladen F, Liu H, Niggemann B, Fang Q, Zaenker KS et al. Boswellic acid acetate induces differentiation and apoptosis in highly metastatic melanoma and fibrosarcoma cells. Cancer Detect Prev 2003;27:67-75.

127. Syrovets T, Gschwend JE, Buchele B, Laumonnier Y, Zugmaier W, Genze F et al. Inhibition of IkappaB kinase activity by acetyl-boswellic acids promotes apoptosis in androgen-independent PC-3 prostate cancer cells in vitro and in vivo. J Biol Chem 2005;280:6170-80.

128. Xia L, Chen D, Han R, Fang Q, Waxman S, Jing Y. Boswellic acid acetate induces apoptosis through caspase-mediated pathways in myeloid leukemia cells. Mol.Cancer Ther 2005;4:381-88.

129. Liu JJ, Huang B, Hooi SC. Acetyl-keto-beta-boswellic acid inhibits cellular proliferation through a p21-dependent pathway in colon cancer cells. Br J Pharmacol 2006;148:1099-107.

130. Janssen G, Bode U, Breu H, Dohrn B, Engelbrecht V, Gobel U. Boswellic acids in the palliative therapy of children with progressive or relapsed brain tumors. Klin Padiatr 2000;212:189-95.

131. Streffer JR, Bitzer M, Schabet M, Dichgans J, Weller M. Response of radiochemotherapy-associated cerebral edema to a phytotherapeutic agent, H15. Neurology 2001;56:1219-21.

132. Winking M, Sarikaya S, Rahmanian A, Jodicke A, Boker DK. Boswellic acids inhibit glioma growth: a new treatment option? J Neurooncol 2000;46:97-103.

133. Rose ML, Madren J, Bunzendahl H, Thurman RG. Dietary glycine inhibits the growth of B16 melanoma tumors in mice. Carcinogenesis 1999;20:793-98.

134. Amin K, Li J, Chao WR, Dewhirst MW, Haroon ZA. Dietary glycine inhibits angiogenesis during wound healing and tumor growth. Cancer Biol Ther 2003;2:173-78.

135. McCarty MF. The anti-angiogencic impact of dietary of glycine may be mediated by a hyperpolarization-induced suppression of NADPH oxidase activity. Medical Hypotheses 2007;in press.

136. Nangia-Makker P, Hogan V, Honjo Y, Baccarini S, Tait L, Bresalier R et al. Inhibition of human cancer cell growth and metastasis in nude mice by oral intake of modified citrus pectin. J Natl Cancer Inst 2002;94:1854-62.

137. Takenaka Y, Fukumori T, Raz A. Galectin-3 and metastasis. Glycoconj J 2004;19:543-49.

138. Inufusa H, Nakamura M, Adachi T, Aga M, Kurimoto M, Nakatani Y et al. Role of galectin-3 in adenocarcinoma liver metastasis. Int J Oncol 2001;19:913-19.

139. Inohara H, Raz A. Effects of natural complex carbohydrate (citrus pectin) on murine melanoma cell properties related to galectin-3 functions. Glycoconj J 1994;11:527-32.

140. Nangia-Makker P, Honjo Y, Sarvis R, Akahani S, Hogan V, Pienta KJ et al. Galectin-3 induces endothelial cell morphogenesis and angiogenesis. Am J Pathol 2000;156:899-909.

141. Guess BW, Scholz MC, Strum SB, Lam RY, Johnson HJ, Jennrich RI. Modified citrus pectin (MCP) increases the prostate-specific antigen doubling time in men with prostate cancer: a phase II pilot study. Prostate Cancer Prostatic Dis 2003;6:301-04.

142. Cao Y, Feng Z, Hoos A, Klimberg VS. Glutamine enhances gut glutathione production. JPEN J Parenter Enteral Nut. 1998;22:224-27.

143. Yoshida S, Kaibara A, Ishibashi N, Shirouzu K. Glutamine supplementation in cancer patients. Nutrition 2001;17:766-68.

144. Jensen JC, Schaefer R, Nwokedi E, Bevans DW, III, Baker ML, Pappas AA et al. Prevention of chronic radiation enteropathy by dietary glutamine. Ann Surg Oncol 1994;1:157-63.

145. Klimberg VS, Souba WW, Dolson DJ, Salloum RM, Hautamaki RD, Plumley DA et al. Prophylactic glutamine protects the intestinal mucosa from radiation injury. Cancer 1990;66:62-68.

146. Scheid C, Hermann K, Kremer G, Holsing A, Heck G, Fuchs M et al. Randomized, double-blind, controlled study of glycyl-glutamine-dipeptide in the parenteral nutrition of patients with acute leukemia undergoing intensive chemotherapy. Nutrition 2004;20:249-54.

147. May PE, Barber A, D'Olimpio JT, Hourihane A, Abumrad NN. Reversal of cancer-related wasting using oral supplementation with a combination of beta-hydroxy-beta-methylbutyrate, arginine, and glutamine. Am J Surg 2002;183:471-79.

148. Matthews NE, Adams MA, Maxwell LR, Gofton TE, Graham CH. Nitric oxide-mediated regulation of chemosensitivity in cancer cells. J Natl Cancer Inst 2001;93:1879-85.

149. Frederiksen LJ, Siemens DR, Heaton JP, Maxwell LR, Adams MA, Graham CH. Hypoxia induced resistance to doxorubicin in prostate cancer cells is inhibited by low concentrations of glyceryl trinitrate. J Urol 2003;170:1003-07.

150. Muir CP, Adams MA, Graham CH. Nitric oxide attenuates resistance to doxorubicin in three-dimensional aggregates of human breast carcinoma cells. Breast Cancer Res Treat 2006;96:169-76.

151. Frederiksen LJ, Sullivan R, Maxwell LR, Macdonald-Goodfellow SK, Adams MA, Bennett BM et al. Chemosensitization of cancer in vitro and in vivo by nitric oxide signaling. Clin Cancer Res 2007;13:2199-206.

152. Whorton AR, Simonds DB, Piantadosi CA. Regulation of nitric oxide synthesis by oxygen in vascular endothelial cells. Am J Physiol 1997;272:L1161-L1166.

153. McCormick CC, Li WP, Calero M. Oxygen tension limits nitric oxide synthesis by activated macrophages. Biochem J 2000;350 Pt 3:709-16.

154. Vesely DL. Biotin enhances guanylate cyclase activity. Science 1982;216:1329-30.

Chapter Eleven – IRT Nutraceuticals for Specific Cancers

1. Kuiper GG, Enmark E, Pelto-Huikko M, Nilsson S, Gustafsson JA. Cloning of a novel receptor expressed in rat prostate and ovary. Proc Natl Acad Sci USA 1996;93:5925-30.

2. McCarty MF. Isoflavones made simple - genistein's agonist activity for the beta-type estrogen receptor mediates their health benefits. Med Hypotheses 2006;66:1093-114.

3. Fixemer T, Remberger K, Bonkhoff H. Differential expression of the estrogen receptor beta (ERbeta) in human prostate tissue, premalignant changes, and in primary, metastatic, and recurrent prostatic adenocarcinoma. Prostate 2003;54:79-87.

4. Jassam N, Bell SM, Speirs V, Quirke P. Loss of expression of oestrogen receptor beta in colon cancer and its association with Dukes' staging. Oncol Rep 2005;14:17-21.

5. Konstantinopoulos PA, Kominea A, Vandoros G, Sykiotis GP, Andricopoulos P, Varakis I et al. Oestrogen receptor beta (ERbeta) is abundantly expressed in normal colonic mucosa, but declines in colon adenocarcinoma paralleling the tumour's dedifferentiation. Eur J Cancer 2003;39:1251-58.

6. Royuela M, de Miguel MP, Bethencourt FR, Sanchez-Chapado M, Fraile B, Arenas MI et al. Estrogen receptors alpha and beta in the normal, hyperplastic and carcinomatous human prostate. J Endocrinol 2001;168:447-54.

7. Lau KM, LaSpina M, Long J, Ho SM. Expression of estrogen receptor (ER)-alpha and ER-beta in normal and malignant prostatic epithelial cells: regulation by methylation and involvement in growth regulation. Cancer Res 2000;60:3175-82.

8. Wada-Hiraike O, Warner M, Gustafsson JA. New developments in oestrogen signalling in colonic epithelium. Biochem Soc Tran. 2006;34:1114-16.

9. Xie LQ, Yu JP, Luo HS. Expression of estrogen receptor beta in human colorectal cancer. World J Gastroenterol 2004;10:214-17.

10. Witte D, Chirala M, Younes A, Li Y, Younes M. Estrogen receptor beta is expressed in human colorectal adenocarcinoma. Hum Pathol 2001;32:940-44.

11. Bardin A, Hoffmann P, Boulle N, Katsaros D, Vignon F, Pujol P et al. Involvement of estrogen receptor beta in ovarian carcinogenesis. Cancer Res 2004;64:5861-69.

12. Chen X, Anderson JJ. Isoflavones inhibit proliferation of ovarian cancer cells in vitro via an estrogen receptor-dependent pathway. Nutr Cancer 2001;41:165-71.

13. Chlebowski RT, Wactawski-Wende J, Ritenbaugh C, Hubbell FA, Ascensao J, Rodabough RJ et al. Estrogen plus progestin and colorectal cancer in postmenopausal women. N Engl J Med 2004;350:991-1004.

14. Kurahashi N, Iwasaki M, Sasazuki S, Otani T, Inoue M, Tsugane S. Soy product and isoflavone consumption in relation to prostate cancer in Japanese men. Cancer Epidemiol. Biomarkers Prev 2007;16:538-45.

15. Cotterchio M, Boucher BA, Manno M, Gallinger S, Okey A, Harper P. Dietary phytoestrogen intake is associated with reduced colorectal cancer risk. J Nutr 2006;136:3046-53.

16. Zhang M, Xie X, Lee AH, Binns CW. Soy and isoflavone intake are associated with reduced risk of ovarian cancer in southeast china. Nutr Cancer 2004;49:125-30.

17. Hikosaka A, Asamoto M, Hokaiwado N, Kato K, Kuzutani K, Kohri K et al. Inhibitory effects of soy isoflavones on rat prostate carcinogenesis induced by 2-amino-1-methyl-6-phenylimidazo[4,5-b]pyridine (PhIP). Carcinogenesis 2004;25:381-87.

18. Guo JY, Li X, Browning JD, Jr., Rottinghaus GE, Lubahn DB, Constantinou A et al. Dietary soy isoflavones and estrone protect ovariectomized ERalphaKO and wild-type mice from carcinogen-induced colon cancer. J Nutr 2004;134:179-82.

19. Tanaka T, Kohno H, Tanino M, Yanaida Y. Inhibitory effects of estrogenic compounds, 4-nonylphenol and genistein, on 7,12-dimethylbenz[a]anthracene-induced ovarian carcinogenesis in rats. Ecotoxicol Environ Saf 2002;52:38-45.

20. Raffoul JJ, Banerjee S, Singh-Gupta V, Knoll ZE, Fite A, Zhang H et al. Down-regulation of apurinic/apyrimidinic endonuclease 1/redox factor-1 expression by soy isoflavones enhances prostate cancer radiotherapy in vitro and in vivo. Cancer Res 2007;67:2141-49.

21. Maskarinec G, Morimoto Y, Hebshi S, Sharma S, Franke AA, Stanczyk FZ. Serum prostate-specific antigen but not testosterone levels decrease in a randomized soy intervention among men. Eur J Clin Nutr 2006;60:1423-29.

22. Giovannucci E. A review of epidemiologic studies of tomatoes, lycopene, and prostate cancer. Exp Biol Med (Maywood) 2002;227:852-59.

23. Tang L, Jin T, Zeng X, Wang JS. Lycopene inhibits the growth of human androgen-independent prostate cancer cells in vitro and in BALB/c nude mice. J Nutr 2005;135:287-90.

24. Ansari MS, Gupta NP. Lycopene: a novel drug therapy in hormone refractory metastatic prostate cancer. Urol Oncol 2004;22:415-20.

25. Ansari MS, Gupta NP. A comparison of lycopene and orchidectomy vs orchidectomy alone in the management of advanced prostate cancer. BJU Int 2003;92:375-78.

26. Schroder FH, Roobol MJ, Boeve ER, de Mutsert R, Zuijdgeest-van Leeuwen SD, Kersten I et al. Randomized, double-blind, placebo-controlled crossover study in men with prostate cancer and rising PSA: effectiveness of a dietary supplement. Eur Urol 2005;48:922-30.

27. Chen L, Stacewicz-Sapuntzakis M, Duncan C, Sharifi R, Ghosh L, van Breemen R et al. Oxidative DNA damage in prostate cancer patients consuming tomato sauce-based entrees as a whole-food intervention. J NatlCancer Inst 2001;93:1872-79.

28. Albrecht M, Jiang W, Kumi-Diaka J, Lansky EP, Gommersall LM, Patel A et al. Pomegranate extracts potently suppress proliferation, xenograft growth, and invasion of human prostate cancer cells. J Med Food 2004;7:274-83.

29. Malik A, Afaq F, Sarfaraz S, Adhami VM, Syed DN, Mukhtar H. Pomegranate fruit juice for chemoprevention and chemotherapy of prostate cancer. Proc Natl Acad Sci USA 2005;102:14813-18.

30. Pantuck AJ, Leppert JT, Zomorodian N, Aronson W, Hong J, Barnard RJ et al. Phase II study of pomegranate juice for men with rising prostate-specific antigen following surgery or radiation for prostate cancer. Clin Cancer Res 2006;12:4018-26.

31. Khan N, Hadi N, Afaq F, Syed DN, Kweon MH, Mukhtar H. Pomegranate fruit extract inhibits prosurvival pathways in human A549 lung carcinoma cells and tumor growth in athymic nude mice. Carcinogenesis 2007;28:163-73.

32. Khan N, Afaq F, Kweon MH, Kim K, Mukhtar H. Oral consumption of pomegranate fruit extract inhibits growth and progression of primary lung tumors in mice. Cancer Res 2007;67:3475-82.

33. Casey AC, Bliznakov EG. Effect and structure-activity relationship of the coenzymes Q on the phagocytic rate of rats. Chem Biol Interact 1972;5:1-12.

34. Bliznakov E, Casey A, Premuzic E. Coenzymes Q: stimulants of the phagocytic activity in rats and immune response in mice. Experientia 1970;26:953-54.

35. Lockwood K, Moesgaard S, Folkers K. Partial and complete regression of breast cancer in patients in relation to dosage of coenzyme Q10. Biochem Biophys Res Commun 1994;199:1504-08.

36. Lockwood K, Moesgaard S, Yamamoto T, Folkers K. Progress on therapy of breast cancer with vitamin Q10 and the regression of metastases. Biochem Biophys Res Commun 1995;212:172-77.

37. Folkers K, Osterborg A, Nylander M, Morita M, Mellstedt H. Activities of vitamin Q10 in animal models and a serious deficiency in patients with cancer. Biochem Biophys Res Commun 1997;234:296-99.

38. Garvin S, Ollinger K, Dabrosin C. Resveratrol induces apoptosis and inhibits angiogenesis in human breast cancer xenografts in vivo. Cancer Lett 2006;231:113-22.

Chapter Twelve – IRT Specific Drugs for Cancer Control

1. Tonnesen H, Knigge U, Bulow S, Damm P, Fischerman K, Hesselfeldt P, Hjortrup A, Pedersen IK, Pedersen VM, Siemssen OJ, . Effect of cimetidine on survival after gastric cancer. Lancet 1988 October 29;2(8618):990-2.

2. Svendsen LB, Ross C, Knigge U, Frederiksen HJ, Graversen P, Kjaergard J, Luke M, Stimpel H, Sparso BH. Cimetidine as an adjuvant treatment in colorectal cancer. A double-blind, randomized pilot study. Dis Colon Rectum 1995 May;38(5):514-8.

3. Matsumoto S, Imaeda Y, Umemoto S, Kobayashi K, Suzuki H, Okamoto T. Cimetidine increases survival of colorectal cancer patients with high levels of sialyl Lewis-X and sialyl Lewis-A epitope expression on tumour cells. Br J Cancer 2002 January; 21;86(2):161-7.

4. Morton RF, Creagan ET, Cullinan SA, Mailliard JA, Ebbert L, Veeder MH, Chang M. Phase II studies of single-agent cimetidine and the combination N-phosphonacetyl-L-aspartate (NSC-224131) plus L-alanosine (NSC-153353) in advanced malignant melanoma. J Clin Oncol 1987 July;5(7):1078-82.

5. Inhorn L, Williams SD, Nattam S, Stephens D. High-dose cimetidine for the treatment of metastatic renal cell carcinoma. A Hoosier Oncology Group study. Am J Clin Oncol 1992 April;15(2):157-9.

6. Natori T, Sata M, Nagai R, Makuuchi M. Cimetidine inhibits angiogenesis and suppresses tumor growth. Biomed Pharmacother 2005 January;59(1-2):56-60.

7. Lefranc F, James S, Camby I, Gaussin JF, Darro F, Brotchi J, Gabius J, Kiss R. Combined cimetidine and temozolomide, compared with temozolomide alone: significant increases in survival in nude mice bearing U373 human glioblastoma multiforme orthotopic xenografts. J Neurosurg 2005 April;102(4):706-14.

8. Primrose JN, Miller GV, Preston SR, Gokhale J, Ambrose NS, Ward UM, Mills JG, Ehsanullah RS, Darekar B. A prospective randomised controlled study of the use of ranitidine in patients with gastric cancer. Yorkshire GI Tumour Group. Gut 1998 January;42(1):17-9.

9. Nielsen HJ, Christensen IJ, Moesgaard F, Kehlet H. Ranitidine as adjuvant treatment in colorectal cancer. Br J Surg 2002 November;89(11):1416-22.

10 Kobayashi K, Matsumoto S, Morishima T, Kawabe T, Okamoto T. Cimetidine inhibits cancer cell adhesion to endothelial cells and prevents metastasis by blocking E-selectin expression. Cancer Res 2000 July 15;60(14):3978-84.

11. Kannagi R, Izawa M, Koike T, Miyazaki K, Kimura N. Carbohydrate-mediated cell adhesion in cancer metastasis and angiogenesis. Cancer Sci 2004 May;95(5):377-84.

12. Adams WJ, Morris DL. Short-course cimetidine and survival with colorectal cancer. Lancet 1994 December 24;344(8939-8940):1768-9.

13. Natori T, Sata M, Nagari R, Makuuchi M. Cimetidine inhibits angiogenesis and suppresses tumor growth. Biomed Pharmacother 2005 January;59(1-2):56-60.

14. Aoki M, Kanamori M, Yudoh K, Ohmori K, Yasuda T, Kimura T. Effects of vascular endothelial growth factor and E-selectin on angiogenesis in the murine metastatic RCT sarcoma. Tumour Biol 2001 July;22(4):239-46.

15. Garcia Rodriguez LA, Jick H. Risk of gynaecomastia associated with cimetidine, omeprazole, and other antiulcer drugs. BMJ 1994 February 19;308(6927):503-6.

15. Marks PA, Dokmanovic M. Histone deacetylase inhibitors: discovery and development as anticancer agents. Expert Opin Investig Drugs 2005;14:1497-511.

17. Liu T, Kuljaca S, Tee A, Marshall GM. Histone deacetylase inhibitors: multifunctional anticancer agents. Cancer Treat Rev 2006;32:157-65.

18. Zhang X, Yashiro M, Ren J, Hirakawa K. Histone deacetylase inhibitor, trichostatin A, increases the chemosensitivity of anticancer drugs in gastric cancer cell lines. Oncol Rep 2006;16:563-68.

19. Kim MS, Blake M, Baek JH, Kohlhagen G, Pommier Y, Carrier F. Inhibition of histone deacetylase increases cytotoxicity to anticancer drugs targeting DNA. Cancer Res 2003;63:7291-300.

20. Zhang Y, Jung M, Dritschilo A, Jung M. Enhancement of radiation sensitivity of human squamous carcinoma cells by histone deacetylase inhibitors. Radiat Res 2004;161:667-74.

21. Camphausen K, Cerna D, Scott T, Sproull M, Burgan WE, Cerra MA et al. Enhancement of in vitro and in vivo tumor cell radiosensitivity by valproic acid. Int J Cancer 2005;114:380-86.

22. Cerna D, Camphausen K, Tofilon PJ. Histone deacetylation as a target for radiosensitization. Curr Top Dev Biol 2006;73:173-204.

23. Marks PA, Jiang X. Histone deacetylase inhibitors in programmed cell death and cancer therapy. Cell Cycle 2005;4:549-51.

24. Deroanne CF, Bonjean K, Servotte S, Devy L, Colige A, Clausse N et al. Histone deacetylases inhibitors as anti-angiogenic agents altering vascular endothelial growth factor signaling. Oncogene 2002;21:427-36.

25. Michaelis M, Michaelis UR, Fleming I, Suhan T, Cinatl J, Blaheta RA et al. Valproic acid inhibits angiogenesis in vitro and in vivo. Mol Pharmacol 2004;65:520-27.

26. Kwon HJ, Kim MS, Kim MJ, Nakajima H, Kim KW. Histone deacetylase inhibitor FK228 inhibits tumor angiogenesis. Int J Cancer 2002;97:290-96.

27. Zgouras D, Becker U, Loitsch S, Stein J. Modulation of angiogenesis-related protein synthesis by valproic acid. Biochem Biophys Res Commun 2004;316:693-97.

28. Fath DM, Kong X, Liang D, Lin Z, Chou A, Jiang Y et al. Histone deacetylase inhibitors repress the transactivation potential of hypoxia-inducible factors independently of direct acetylation of HIF-alpha. J Biol Chem 2006;281:13612-19.

29. Qian DZ, Kachhap SK, Collis SJ, Verheul HM, Carducci MA, Atadja P et al. Class II Histone Deacetylases Are Associated with VHL-Independent Regulation of Hypoxia-Inducible Factor 1{alpha}. Cancer Res 2006;66:8814-21.

30. Armeanu S, Bitzer M, Lauer UM, Venturelli S, Pathil A, Krusch M et al. Natural killer cell-mediated lysis of hepatoma cells via specific induction of NKG2D ligands by the histone deacetylase inhibitor sodium valproate. Cancer Res 2005;65:6321-29.

31. Gottlicher M, Minucci S, Zhu P, Kramer OH, Schimpf A, Giavara S et al. Valproic acid defines a novel class of HDAC inhibitors inducing differentiation of transformed cells. EMBO J 2001;20:6969-78.

32. Gottlicher M. Valproic acid: an old drug newly discovered as inhibitor of histone deacetylases. Ann Hematol 2004;83 Suppl 1:S91-S92.

33. Marks PA, Richon VM, Miller T, Kelly WK. Histone deacetylase inhibitors. Adv Cancer Res 2004;91:137-68.

34. Catalano MG, Fortunati N, Pugliese M, Costantino L, Poli R, Bosco O et al. Valproic acid induces apoptosis and cell cycle arrest in poorly differentiated thyroid cancer cells. J Clin Endocrinol Metab 2005;90:1383-89.

35. Morotti A, Cilloni D, Messa F, Arruga F, Defilippi I, Carturan S et al. Valproate enhances imatinib-induced growth arrest and apoptosis in chronic myeloid leukemia cells. Cancer 2006;106:1188-96.

36. Kaiser M, Zavrski I, Sterz J, Jakob C, Fleissner C, Kloetzel PM et al. The effects of the histone deacetylase inhibitor valproic acid on cell cycle, growth suppression and apoptosis in multiple myeloma. Haematologica 2006;91:248-51.

37. Hrzenjak A, Moinfar F, Kremser ML, Strohmeier B, Staber PB, Zatloukal K et al. Valproate inhibition of histone deacetylase 2 affects differentiation and decreases proliferation of endometrial stromal sarcoma cells. Mol Cancer Ther 2006;5:2203-10.

38. Catalano MG, Fortunati N, Pugliese M, Poli R, Bosco O, Mastrocola R et al. Valproic acid, a histone deacetylase inhibitor, enhances sensitivity to doxorubicin in anaplastic thyroid cancer cells. J Endocrinol 2006;191:465-72.

39. Valentini A, Gravina P, Federici G, Bernardini S. Valproic Acid Induces Apoptosis, p(16INK4A) Upregulation and Sensitization to Chemotherapy in Human Melanoma Cells. Cancer Biol Ther 2007;6(2):185-91.

40. Chavez-Blanco A, Segura-Pacheco B, Perez-Cardenas E, Taja-Chayeb L, Cetina L, Candelaria M et al. Histone acetylation and histone deacetylase activity of magnesium valproate in tumor and peripheral blood of patients with cervical cancer. A phase I study. Mol.Cancer. 2005;4:22.

41. Berry J. Are all aromatase inhibitors the same? A review of controlled clinical trials in breast cancer. Clin Ther 2005 November;27(11):1671-84.

42. Moreau JP, Delavault P, Blumberg J. Luteinizing hormone-releasing hormone agonists in the treatment of prostate cancer: a review of their discovery, development, and place in therapy. Clin Ther 2006 October;28(10):1485-508.

43. Bong GW, Clarke HS, Jr., Hancock WC, Keane TE. Serum Testosterone Recovery After Cessation of Long-Term Luteinizing Hormone-Releasing Hormone Agonist in Patients with Prostate Cancer. Urology 2008 February 14.

Chapter Thirteen - Surgery and Radiation Therapy at Oasis of Hope

1. Weinmann M, Welz S, Bamberg M. Hypoxic radiosensitizers and hypoxic cytotoxins in radiation oncology. Curr Med Chem Anticancer Agents 2003 September;3(5):364-74.

2. Maevsky E, Ivanitsky G, Bogdanova L, Axenova O, Karmen N, Zhiburt E, Senina R, Pushkin S, Maslennikov I, Orlov A, Marinicheva I. Clinical results of Perftoran application: present and future. Artif Cells Blood Substit Immobil Biotechnol 2005;33(1):37-46.

3. Wakasa T, Kawai N, Yanagi Y, Hayase Y, Kishi K. A study of hypoxic cell radiosensitizer applied to Ehrlich ascite tumour: a comparison of FC43 emulsion and pentoxyfilline. Br J Radiol 2002 November;75(899):909-12.

4. Lee I, Biaglow JE, Lee J, Cho MJ. Physiological mechanisms of radiation sensitization by pentoxifylline. Anticancer Res 2000 November;20(6B):4605-9.

5. Bocci V, Larini A, Micheli V. Restoration of normoxia by ozone therapy may control neoplastic growth: a review and a working hypothesis. J Altern Complement Med 2005 April;11(2):257-65.

6. Teicher BA. Hypoxia and drug resistance. Cancer Metastasis Rev 1994 June;13(2):139-68.

7. McCarty MF, Barroso-Aranda J, Contreras F. A two-phase strategy for treatment of oxidant-dependent cancers. Med Hypotheses 2007;69(3):489-96.

8. Kopp E, Ghosh S. Inhibition of NF-kappa B by sodium salicylate and aspirin. Science 1994 August 12;265(5174):956-9.

9. Yin MJ, Yamamoto Y, Gaynor RB. The anti-inflammatory agents aspirin and salicylate inhibit the activity of I(kappa)B kinase-beta. Nature 1998 November 5;396(6706):77-80.

10. Dhanalakshmi S, Singh RP, Agarwal C, Agarwal R. Silibinin inhibits constitutive and TNFalpha-induced activation of NF-kappaB and sensitizes human prostate carcinoma DU145 cells to TNFalpha-induced apoptosis. Oncogene 2002 March 7;21(11):1759-67.

11. Singh RP, Mallikarjuna GU, Sharma G, Dhanalakshmi S, Tyagi AK, Chan DC, Agarwal C, Agarwal R. Oral silibinin inhibits lung tumor growth in athymic nude mice and forms a novel chemocombination with doxorubicin targeting nuclear factor kappaB-mediated inducible chemoresistance. Clin Cancer Res 2004 December 15;10(24):8641-7.

12. Magne N, Toillon RA, Bottero V, Didelot C, Houtte PV, Gerard JP, Peyron JF. NF-kappaB modulation and ionizing radiation: mechanisms and future directions for cancer treatment. Cancer Lett 2006 January 18;231(2):158-68.

13. Sundaram S, Gewirtz DA. The vitamin D3 analog EB 1089 enhances the response of human breast tumor cells to radiation. Radiat Res 1999 November;152(5):479-86.

14. Demasters G, Di X, Newsham I, Shiu R, Gewirtz DA. Potentiation of radiation sensitivity in breast tumor cells by the vitamin D3 analogue, EB 1089, through promotion of autophagy and interference with proliferative recovery. Mol Cancer Ther 2006 November;5(11):2786-97.

15. Erbil Y, Oztezcan S, Giris M, Barbaros U, Olgac V, Bilge H, Kucucuk H, Toker G. The effect of glutamine on radiation-induced organ damage. Life Sci 2005 December 12;78(4):376-82.

16. Salman B, Oguz M, Akmansu M, Bebitoglu I, Akca G, Sultan N, Emre U, Kerem M, Yilmaz U. Effect of timing of glutamine-enriched enteral nutrition on intestinal damage caused by irradiation. Adv Ther 2007 May;24(3):648-61.

17. Adams WJ, Morris DL. Short-course cimetidine and survival with colorectal cancer. Lancet 1994 December 24;344(8939-8940):1768-9.

18. Kobayashi K, Matsumoto S, Morishima T, Kawabe T, Okamoto T. Cimetidine inhibits cancer cell adhesion to endothelial cells and prevents metastasis by blocking E-selectin expression. Cancer Res 2000 July 15;60(14):3978-84.

19. Matsumoto S, Imaeda Y, Umemoto S, Kobayashi K, Suzuki H, Okamoto T. Cimetidine increases survival of colorectal cancer patients with high levels of sialyl Lewis-X and sialyl Lewis-A epitope expression on tumour cells. Br J Cancer 2002 January 21;86(2):161-7.

20. Pierce JW, Read MA, Ding H, Luscinskas FW, Collins T. Salicylates inhibit I kappa B-alpha phosphorylation, endothelial-leukocyte adhesion molecule expression, and neutrophil transmigration. J Immunol 1996 May 15;156(10):3961-9.

21. Miller SC, Pandi-Perumal SR, Esquifino AI, Cardinali DP, Maestroni GJ. The role of melatonin in immuno-enhancement: potential application in cancer. Int J Exp Pathol 2006 April;87(2):81-7.

22. Hawkes WC, Kelley DS, Taylor PC. The effects of dietary selenium on the immune system in healthy men. Biol Trace Elem Res 2001 September;81(3):189-213.

23. Verdin-Vasquez RC, Zepeda-Perez C, Ferra-Ferrer R, Chavez-Negrete A, Contreras F, Barroso-Aranda J. Use of perftoran emulsion to decrease allogeneic blood transfusion in cardiac surgery: clinical trial. Artif Cells Blood Substit Immobil Biotechnol 2006;34(4):433-54.

Chapter Fourteen –
Oasis of Hope Diet and Exercise Strategies

1. McCarty MF. Insulin and IGF-I as determinants of low "Western" cancer rates in the rural third world. Int J Epidemiol 2004 August;33(4):908-10.

2. Giovannuci E. Nutrition, insulin, insulin-like growth factors and cancer. Horm Metab Res 2003 November;35(11-12):694-704.

3. Valentinis B, Baserga R. IGF-I receptor signalling in transformation and differentiation. Mol Pathol 2001 June;54(3):133-7.

4. Scott CD, Baxter RC. Production of insulin-like growth factor I and its binding protein in rat hepatocytes cultured from diabetic and insulin-treated diabetic rats. Endocrinology 1986 November;119(5):2346-52.

5. Jousse C, Bruhat A, Ferrara M, Fafournoux P. Physiological concentration of amino acids regulates insulin-like- growth-factor-binding protein 1 expression. Biochem J 1998 August 15;334 (Pt 1):147-53.

6. Allen NE, Appleby PN, Davey GK, Kaaks R, Rinaldi S, Key TJ. The associations of diet with serum insulin-like growth factor I and its main binding proteins in 292 women meat-eaters, vegetarians, and vegans. Cancer Epidemiol Biomarkers Prev 2002 November;11(11):1441-8.

7. Campbell TC, Junshi C. Diet and chronic degenerative diseases: perspectives from China. Am J Clin Nutr 1994 May;59(5 Suppl):1153S-61S.

8. Campbell TC, Campbell TM. The China study : The most comprehensive study of nutrition ever conducted and the startling Implications for diet, weight Loss and long-term health. Benbella Books; 2006.

9. Hiney JK, Srivastava V, Nyberg CL, Ojeda SR, Dees WL. Insulin-like growth factor I of peripheral origin acts centrally to accelerate the initiation of female puberty. Endocrinology 1996 September;137(9):3717-28.

10. Key TJ, Chen J, Wang DY, Pike MC, Boreham J. Sex hormones in women in rural China and in Britain. Br J Cancer 1990 October;62(4):631-6.

11. Meseguer A, Puche C, Cabero A. Sex steroid biosynthesis in white adipose tissue. Horm Metab Res 2002 November;34(11-12):731-6.

12. Baserga R. The insulin-like growth factor-I receptor as a target for cancer therapy. Expert Opin Ther Targets 2005 August;9(4):753-68.

13. Ngo TH, Barnard RJ, Leung PS, Cohen P, Aronson WJ. Insulin-like growth factor I (IGF-I) and IGF binding protein-1 modulate prostate cancer cell growth and apoptosis: possible mediators for the effects of diet and exercise on cancer cell survival. Endocrinology 2003 June;144(6):2319-24.

14. Barnard RJ, Ngo TH, Leung PS, Aronson WJ, Golding LA. A low-fat diet and/or strenuous exercise alters the IGF axis in vivo and reduces prostate tumor cell growth in vitro. Prostate 2003 August 1;56(3):201-6.

15. Barnard RJ, Gonzalez JH, Liva ME, Ngo TH. Effects of a low-fat, high-fiber diet and exercise program on breast cancer risk factors in vivo and tumor cell growth and apoptosis in vitro. Nutr Cancer 2006;55(1):28-34.

16. Ornish D, Weidner G, Fair WR, Marlin R, Pettengill EB, Raisin CJ, Dunn-Emke S, Crutchfield L, Jacobs FN, Barnard RJ, Aronson WJ, McCormac P, McKnight DJ, Fein JD, Dnistrian AM, Weinstein J, Ngo TH, Mendell NR, Carroll PR. Intensive lifestyle changes may affect the progression of prostate cancer. J Urol 2005 September;174(3):1065-9.

17. Borugian MJ, Sheps SB, Kim-Sing C, Olivotto IA, Van Patten C, Dunn BP, Coldman AJ, Potter JD, Gallagher RP, Hislop TG. Waist-to-hip ratio and breast cancer mortality. Am J Epidemiol 2003 November 15;158(10):963-8.

18. Pasanisi P, Berrino F, De PM, Venturelli E, Mastroianni A, Panico S. Metabolic syndrome as a prognostic factor for breast cancer recurrences. Int J Cancer 2006 July 1;119(1):236-8.

19. Holmes MD, Chen WY, Feskanich D, Kroenke CH, Colditz GA. Physical activity and survival after breast cancer diagnosis. JAMA 2005 May 25;293(20):2479-86.

20. Meyerhardt JA, Heseltine D, Niedzwiecki D, Hollis D, Saltz LB, Mayer RJ, Thomas J, Nelson H, Whittom R, Hantel A, Schilsky RL, Fuchs CS. Impact of physical activity on cancer recurrence and survival in patients with stage III colon cancer: findings from CALGB 89803. J Clin Oncol 2006 August 1;24(22):3535-41.

21. Meyerhardt JA, Giovannucci EL, Holmes MD, Chan AT, Chan JA, Colditz GA, Fuchs CS. Physical activity and survival after colorectal cancer diagnosis. J Clin Oncol 2006 August 1;24(22):3527-34.

22. Hutnick NA, Williams NI, Kraemer WJ, Orsega-Smith E, Dixon RH, Bleznak AD, Mastro AM. Exercise and lymphocyte activation following chemotherapy for breast cancer. Med Sci Sports Exerc 2005 November;37(11):1827-35.

23. Quist M, Rorth M, Zacho M, Andersen C, Moeller T, Midtgaard J, Adamsen L. High-intensity resistance and cardiovascular training improve physical capacity in cancer patients undergoing chemotherapy. Scand J Med Sci Sports 2006 October;16(5):349-57.

24. Bahadori B, Pestemer-Lach I. Die 7 Stufen zum Gleichgewicht. 3rd ed. Graz, Austria: Eigenverlag Bahadori; 2005.

25. Perez-Jimenez F, Lopez-Miranda J, Pinillos MD, Gomez P, Paz-Rojas E, Montilla P, Marin C, Velasco MJ, Blanco-Molina A, Jimenez Pereperez JA, Ordovas JM. A Mediterranean and a high-carbohydrate diet improve glucose metabolism in healthy young persons. Diabetologia 2001 November;44(11):2038-43.

26. Sierksma A, Patel H, Ouchi N, Kihara S, Funahashi T, Heine RJ, Grobbee DE, Kluft C, Hendriks HF. Effect of Moderate Alcohol Consumption on Adiponectin, Tumor Necrosis Factor-alpha, and Insulin Sensitivity. Diabetes Care 2004 January;27(1):184-9.

27. Lavigne JA, Baer DJ, Wimbrow HH, Albert PS, Brown ED, Judd JT, Campbell WS, Giffen CA, Dorgan JF, Hartman TJ, Barrett JC, Hursting SD, Taylor PR. Effects of alcohol on insulin-like growth factor I and insulin-like growth factor binding protein 3 in postmenopausal women. Am J Clin Nutr 2005 February;81(2):503-7.

28. Rojdmark S, Rydvald Y, Aquilonius A, Brismar K. Insulin-like growth factor (IGF)-1 and IGF-binding protein-1 concentrations in serum of normal subjects after alcohol ingestion: evidence for decreased IGF-1 bioavailability. Clin Endocrinol (Oxf) 2000 March;52(3):313-8.

29. Farchi G, Fidanza F, Giampaoli S, Mariotti S, Menotti A. Alcohol and survival in the Italian rural cohorts of the Seven Countries Study. Int J Epidemiol 2000 August;29(4):667-71.

30. Byles J, Young A, Furuya H, Parkinson L. A drink to healthy aging: The association between older women's use of alcohol and their health-related quality of life. J Am Geriatr Soc 2006 September;54(9):1341-7.

31. Keum YS, Jeong WS, Kong AN. Chemopreventive functions of isothiocyanates. Drug News Perspect 2005 September;18(7):445-51.

32. Munday R, Munday CM. Induction of phase II enzymes by aliphatic sulfides derived from garlic and onions: an overview. Methods Enzymol 2004;382:449-56.

33. McCarty MF. "Iatrogenic Gilbert sydrome" - a strategy for reducing vascular and cancer risk by increasing plasma unconjugated bilirubin. Medical Hypotheses 2007;accepted for publication.

34. McCarty MF. Clinical potential of spirulina as a source of phycocyanobilin. J Medicinal Food 2007;in press.

35. McCarty MF, Barroso-Aranda J, Contreras F. A two-phase strategy for treatment of oxidant-dependent cancers. Med Hypotheses 2007 May 12.

36. Brar SS, Kennedy TP, Quinn M, Hoidal JR. Redox signaling of NF-kappaB by membrane NAD(P)H oxidases in normal and malignant cells. Protoplasma 2003 May;221(1-2):117-27.

37. Wu WS. The signaling mechanism of ROS in tumor progression. Cancer Metastasis Rev 2006 December;25(4):695-705.

38. Ushio-Fukai M. Redox signaling in angiogenesis: role of NADPH oxidase. Cardiovasc Res 2006 July 15;71(2):226-35.

39. Ushio-Fukai M. VEGF signaling through NADPH oxidase-derived ROS. Antioxid Redox Signal 2007 June;9(6):731-9.

40. Pugh N, Ross SA, ElSohly HN, ElSohly MA, Pasco DS. Isolation of three high molecular weight polysaccharide preparations with potent immunostimulatory activity from Spirulina platensis, aphanizomenon flos-aquae and Chlorella pyrenoidosa. Planta Med 2001 November;67(8):737-42.

Chapter Fifteen – Emotional Support at Oasis of Hope

1. Fulcher CD, Badger T, Gunter AK, Marrs J, Reese JM. Putting Evidence into Practice: Interventions for Depression. Clin J Oncology Nursing, Vol 12(1), 2008, 131-140.

2. Sternberg EM. The Balance Within. The Science Connecting Health and Emotions. W. H. Freeman and Company: New York, 2001.

3. Salovey P, Rothman AJ, Detweiler JB. Emotional States and Physical Health. American Psychologist, Vol 55(1), Jan 2000, 110-121.

4. Le Shan L. Psychological States as Factors in the Development of Malignant Disease: A Critical Review. Journal of the National Cancer Institute, Vol 22, 1959, 1-18.

5. Eysenck HJ. Personality, Stress and Cancer. British Journal of Medical Psychology, Vol 61, 1988, 57.

6. Le Shan L, Worthington RE. Some Recurrent Life History Patterns Observed in Patients with Malignant Disease. Journal Nerv. of Mental Disease, Vol 124, 1956, 460-465.

7. Cooper GL. Stress, Medicine and Health. CRC Press: New York, 1996

8. Appelhans BM, Luecken LJ. Heart Rate Variability as an Index of Regulated Emotional Responding. Review of General Psychology, Vol 10(3), Sep 2006, 229-240.

9. Martin P. The Healing Mind: The Vital Links Between Brain and Behavior, Immunity and Disease. Thomas Dunne: New York, 1999.

10. Mahoney S. This is Your Brain on Illness. Prevention, Vol 60(4), 2008.

11. Ray O. How the Mind Hurts and Heals the Body. American Psychologist, Vol 59(1), Jan 2004, 29-40.

12. Pert C, Chopra D. Molecules of Emotion: Why You Feel the Way You Feel. New York: Simon and Schuster, 1999.

13. Cousins, N. Head First: The Biology of Hope and the Healing Power of Human Spirit. New York: Penguin Books, 1990.

14. Crogan NL, Evans BC, Bendel R. Storytelling Interventions for Depression. Oncology Nursing Forum, Vol 35(2), 265-272.

15. Collie K, Kreshka MA, Ferrier S, Parsons R, Graddy K, Avram S, Mannell P, Chen XH, Perkins J, Koopman, C. Videoconferencing for delivery of breast cancer support groups to women living in rural communities: a pilot study. Psycho-Oncology, Vol 16(8), 2007, 778-782.

16. Tacón, A.M., Caldera, Y.M., Ronaghan, C. Mindfulness-Based Stress Reduction in Women With Breast Cancer. Families, Systems, & Health, Vol. 22 (2), Summer 2004, 193-203.

Chapter Sixteen – Caring for the Spirit at Oasis of Hope

1. Schneider MA. Broadening our perspective on spirituality and coping among women with breast cancer and their families: Implications for practice. Indian Journal of Palliative Care, Dec 2007; 13 (2): 25-31.

2. Shaw B, Han JY, Kim E, Gustafson D, Hawkins R, Cleary J, McTavish F, Pingree S, Eliason P, Lumpkins C. Effects of prayer and religious expression within computer support groups on women with breast cancer. Psycho-Oncology, 2007 Jul; 16 (7): 676-87

3. Tarakeshwar N, Vanderwerker LC, Paulk E, Pearce MJ, Kasl SV, Prigerson. Religious coping is associated with the quality of life of patients with advanced cancer. HG Journal of Palliative Medicine, 2006 Jun; 9 (3): 646-57

4. Choumanova I, Wanat S, Barrett R, Koopman C. Religion and spirituality in coping with breast cancer: perspectives of Chilean women. Breast Journal, Jul/Aug 2006; 12 (4): 349-52

5. Meraviglia M. Effects of Spirituality in Breast Cancer Survivors. Oncology Nursing Forum, Jan 2006 Online Exclusive, Vol. 33 Issue 1, pE1-E7, 7p

6. Kernohan WG, Waldron M, McAfee C, Cochrane B, Hasson F. An evidence base for a palliative care chaplaincy service in Northern Ireland. By:. Palliative Medicine, Oct 2006, Vol. 21 Issue 6, p519-525, 7p

For more information:

www.oasisofhope.com
1-888-500-HOPE
(619)-690-8450